Better Homes and Gardens®

1001 DO-IT-YOURSELF TIPS

Better Homes and Gardens® Books
Des Moines

BETTER HOMES AND GARDENS® BOOKS
An Imprint of Meredith® Books

1001 DO-IT-YOURSELF TIPS
Writer/Editor: Linda Mason Hunter
Editor: Benjamin W. Allen
Associate Art Director: Tom Wegner
Electronic Production Coordinator: Paula Forest
Production Manager: Douglas Johnston
Contributing Graphic Designer: Mike Burns
Contributing Illustrator: Carson Ode

Vice President and Editorial Director: Elizabeth P. Rice
Executive Editor: Kay M. Sanders
Art Director: Ernest Shelton
Managing Editor: Christopher Cavanaugh

President, Book Group: Joseph J. Ward
Vice President, Retail Marketing: Jamie L. Martin
Vice President, Direct Marketing: Timothy Jarrell

Meredith Corporation
Chairman of the Executive Committee: E.T. Meredith III
Chairman of the Board and Chief Executive Officer: Jack D. Rehm
President and Chief Operating Officer: William T. Kerr

WE CARE!

All of us at Better Homes and Gardens Books are dedicated to providing you with the information and ideas you need for successful home improvement projects. We guarantee your satisfaction with this book for as long as you own it. We welcome your questions, comments, or suggestions. Please write to us at: Better Homes and Gardens Books, DIY Editorial Department, RW 240, 1716 Locust Street, Des Moines, IA 50309-3023.

If you would like to order additional copies of any of our books, call 1-800-678-2803 or check with your local bookstore.

TABLE OF CONTENTS

You spend Saturday with a paintbrush in hand or on your knees laying a brick patio. You take a vacation to reroof your house. You organize neighborhood gatherings revolving around the delivery of tons of black soil. You're taking part in...

AMERICA'S FAVORITE PASTIME...

and you've got company—lots of it—according to the National Retail Hardware Association (NRHA). The latest NRHA Consumer Profile shows that a whopping 75 million households take part in do-it-yourself projects.

Painting remains the easiest and the most popular activity. How appropriate. After all, the do-it-yourself (DIY) movement began with the development of latex paints in 1948. By 1952, prepasted wallcoverings and drywall filled store shelves. From there the trend steadily accelerated thanks to better products, easier instructions, and how-to magazines. Today, do-it-yourselfers apply 84 percent of all the paint sold, according to the National Decorating Products Association.

But do-it-yourself isn't limited to painting. About 30 percent of DIY households take on major projects.

WHAT CONSTITUTES A MAJOR PROJECT?

It's not necessarily cost or size, but construction skills that determine a project's scope: adding a deck, remodeling a bathroom or kitchen, adding a room, or finishing a basement or attic are considered to be major projects.

Every year 7.5 percent of do-it-yourself households build a deck, and 2.8 million families add a room to their homes.

Although not all major projects are doable (at least not by everyone), no one can tell you what you should or should not attempt. Consider more than your skills or experience—look at the money, time, energy, physical strength, and tools the job requires. Do you have enough of each to finish a project? Will it save you money?

There are ways around a lack of skill if you really want to "do it yourself." Give friends or neighbors a hand with a project in exchange for their help.

NEVER AGAIN

Some projects, such as pouring a large concrete slab, you should never do unless you're an intrepid, well-skilled, do-it-yourselfer. It's hard, back-breaking work unless you do it in little sections and that costs too much. It pays only if you have the mixer make one big pour.

Another headache is hanging drywall in a whole house. The job involves a lot of work and you need two or three people to do it properly—all to save a few hundred dollars. It's not worth it.

CASH IN YOUR POCKET

Which brings up the subject: Do you save money by doing the work? Yes, but how much savings is worth the effort? You save big on labor-intensive jobs such as framing, but not on material-intensive jobs like insulating. Because contractors get discounts on materials, they can probably do some jobs for the same amount or slightly more than it costs you just for materials. That's why it's important to compare costs to determine the best route.

It's wise to do a "do-it-yourself risk/benefit comparison," balancing what you save with your labor against what you might lose because of inexperience or lack of skill. Sometimes doing it yourself doesn't pay, for example:
* If the job requires investment in a lot of tools.
* If the project requires expensive materials.
* If the job requires an expert finish or can be easily damaged.
(continued)

Whatever their skill level, why do do-it-yourselfers do what they do? More than 48 percent of respondents to *Hardware Age* magazine's Consumer Profile said saving money ranks No.1, while 28 percent cite satisfaction. Almost 17 percent gave both reasons. The fact is, people get gratification from hands-on projects. There's a gleam in their eyes when they say, "I did it myself." They're proud of their efforts and achievements.

Sometimes, saving money isn't the issue. It's a matter of getting the job done, especially if it's small. It's often difficult to hire a contractor to make a small repair because a contractor cannot lower costs enough to make the project affordable for you and still make a profit.

Most people begin by doing basic maintenance and repairs and simple decorating and remodeling projects: painting walls, caulking windows,

Also, it's not a good idea to design a major project unless you have a design background. You run the risk of having a project that is well-built but doesn't look right. Hiring a designer is money well spent.

In theory, there is nothing you can't do on your own property; in practice, it's another story. Every major job must meet local building codes, the chief reason your community requires a building permit for major changes or additions. It gives the building inspector a way to review your plans and check your work. You can, for example, add another electrical circuit to your house, but the job requires an electrical permit and must pass inspection before you activate the circuit.

TOP 10 DIY PROJECTS

EASY
1. Interior painting
2. Replacing light switch/outlets
3. Exterior painting
4. Applying weatherstripping or caulk
5. Installing a light fixture
6. Repairing toilet/replacing seat
7. Varnishing or staining wood
8. Replacing door locks
9. Installing bathroom accessories
10. Repairing a screen

MODERATE
1. Installing a ceiling fan
2. Repairing drywall
3. Repairing or replacing roof
4. Installing insulation
5. Installing carpet
6. Laying floor tile
7. Installing storm windows/doors
8. Replacing entrance door
9. Installing gutters/downspouts
10. Paneling a room

MAJOR
1. Remodeling or adding a full bathroom
2. Adding a deck
3. Remodeling a kitchen
4. Enclosing a garage or patio
5. Adding a room
6. Finishing a basement
7. Adding a patio
8. Finishing an attic
9. Installing a skylight
10. Installing a fireplace

1 KEEP REPAIR COSTS DOWN

Neglecting major house maintenance not only affects your enjoyment of your home, it affects the overall value if and when you put your house on the market.

Here are eight common household problems you should nip in the bud to keep home repair costs down. Next to each problem is the damage that can occur if the problem is not corrected early.

1. Faulty roof flashings—Roof leaks and possible structural and cosmetic damage.
2. Malfunctioning gutters—Water damage inside the house.
3. Poor foundation grading—Dampness or water inside the house.
4. Poor tub/shower caulking and grouting—A water leak can spread virtually anywhere, but mainly to the room(s) below the fixture.
5. Damaged bathroom tile—Loose fixtures and/or water leakage to the floor below.
6. Not enough electrical outlets—Overloading of existing outlets and a potential fire hazard.
7. Poor attic ventilation—Roof sheathing rot from excess moisture.
8. Poor mechanical system upkeep—Systems that will not work efficiently or live up to their expected life spans (particularly true for heating and cooling systems). Case in point: Neglecting annual gas furnace inspections could create soot buildup in the flue and result in a chimney fire.

hanging towel bars, installing light fixtures, or replacing faucets.

Confirmed do-it-yourselfers— 39 percent—take on bigger, more complicated projects, such as hanging a new door, laying floor tile, installing a ceiling fan, and repairing drywall.

Then there's that 29.8 percent who will tackle just about anything. These statistics indicate a trend or direction as much as they indicate the number of actual DIY projects. For example, NRHA research shows only 6.4 percent—48 million households—paneled a room in the past year. However, this figure tells you more about paneling as a building material than it does about the

complexity of the job. Paneling has dropped in popularity in the last few years. That means that fewer people hung paneling, but it was for style reasons rather than because it was a difficult job.

Papering a room is another example. NRHA research shows 19.2 percent of do-it-yourself households hung wall covering in their homes, which places the task eleventh on the list of easy activities. However, these do-it-yourselfers hung 70 percent of the wallcovering sold that year, according to The Wallcovering Information Bureau.

2 HOW LONG WILL A DIY JOB TAKE?

How long will a do-it-yourself job take? With average skills and a fair amount of experience, you can add 50 percent to the time a professional would need to finish the job. If you're inexperienced, double or even triple the time.

3 DO-IT-YOURSELF TO SAVE MONEY

Labor accounts for 45 to 60 percent of a remodeling job's cost. Obviously, if you do the work yourself, you can save lots of money.

THE BENCH

PROJECT PRIMER

4 BUILDING A WORKBENCH

Looking for a place to putter? Start by building yourself a sturdy, multipurpose workbench.

Tools: You'll need a tape measure, circular saw, electric drill, and a power screwdriver.

Lumber: Choose the straightest pieces of #1 fir from your local lumberyard or home center. If possible, handpick the straightest pieces.

Fasteners: Drywall screws are easy to drive.

Construct the base before the top. Cut the legs to length and chamfer the bottom edges of the legs so they won't splinter when you drag the bench. Rabbet the top of each leg. (If you want the bench to be flush against the wall as shown, rabbet only one side of the back legs.)

Cut the apron and lay out the pieces with the legs placed inside. (If you have them, bar clamps will help hold the apron in position.) Screw together the framework. Cut the shelf supports and screw together. Cut the shelf, drop in place, and apply the facing.

For the top, you'll need five 2x6s. To equal our overhang you'll need to rip the back board to fit after test fitting the front four 2x6s. Install the cross braces and screw the 1x4 top supports to the cross braces. Assemble the top 2x6s upside down and then flip the framework over and screw the top to the base. Apply two coats of Danish oil.

TOOL SAFETY

5 Always unplug a power tool before servicing or adjustment. Let moving parts come to a standstill before you move near the machine.

6 Never wear loose-fitting clothes or dangling jewelry when using any tools. They could become entangled in motors or gears.

7 Check the condition of a tool before you use it. Inspect power cords for cracks or frays, cutting edges for sharpness, and handles for stability.

8 Don't tamper with or remove safety mechanisms from power tools.

9 Use the proper tool for a job. Read and understand a tool's instruction manual before you use it. Find out what it was meant to do as well as what it can't.

10 If there is even a *remote* possibility of eye injury in a particular situation, wear safety goggles.

11 Keep onlookers, especially children, a safe distance away while you're working with tools. Always instruct others in the proper use of a tool before letting them use it.

12 Work in good light. Use bulbs of sufficient wattage and have extra clamp-on lights so you don't cast a shadow across the project as you work.

13 Never work with tools when you're in a hurry, tired, or in a bad mood.

14 Put tools away after use, preferably in a locked cabinet. Mark tools that need repair before you store them.

MATERIALS LIST

SIZE	AMOUNT	CUTTING LIST
1x4	4 lineal feet	Cut 2 pieces 22¼" for top support
2x6	16 lineal feet	Cut 1 piece 68" and 1 piece 65" for top support
		Cut 2 pieces 23¾" for top support
2x2	3 lineal feet	Cut 2 pieces 15¼" for top support
2x4	20 lineal feet	Cut 2 pieces 22¼" for top support
		Cut 2 pieces 20¾" for bottom shelf support
		Cut 2 pieces 59½" for bottom shelf support
		Cut 1 piece 59½" and rip to ½"x1¼" for shelf facing
2x6	30 lineal feet	Cut 5 pieces 71" for bench top (rip one to 3¼" wide)
4x4	13 lineal feet	Cut 4 pieces 36½" for legs
½" ply	1 4x8 sheet	Cut to 23¼"x58¾"

SUPPLIES: 1½" and 2½" drywall screws, natural Danish oil, and sandpaper

NOTE: Dimensional lumber, such as 2x4s and 1x6s, do not actually measure their named sizes. For example, a 2x4 actually measures 1½x3½".

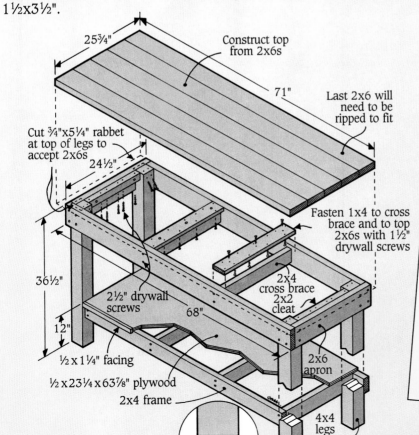

25¾"

Construct top from 2x6s

71"

Last 2x6 will need to be ripped to fit

Cut ¾"x5¼" rabbet at top of legs to accept 2x6s

24½"

Fasten 1x4 to cross brace and to top 2x6s with 1½" drywall screws

36½"

2½" drywall screws

68"

2x4 cross brace
2x2 cleat

12"

½ x 1¼" facing

½ x 23¼ x 63⅞" plywood

2x4 frame

2x6 apron

4x4 legs

Cut bevel at bottom of legs

THE WELL-STOCKED WORKBENCH

Ask 10 do-it-yourselfers what tools they need to outfit a workbench, and you're apt to get 10 different lists. Study the tool inventories closely, however, and you'll find more duplications than differences. With that in mind, here's a look at the basics—plus a few luxuries—for your own well-stocked workbench.

17 Belt sanders These are the perfect tools for quickly smoothing a flat surface. When buying a sander, look for easy-to-use controls, a simple way to remove and install belts, and a belt-tightening system. By selecting a sander with a dust-pickup system, you make breathing easier and cleanup faster.

18 Chalk line Snap a straight line that brushes away after finishing the job.

19 Chisels Bevel-edge chisels in various widths cut wood by chipping it away. Wooden-handle chisels should be struck with a wooden mallet, not a metal hammer.

20 Clamps Use C-clamps to hold pieces together while glue dries. You'll use the 6-inch size most often. Because they can hold large pieces of lumber, pipe and T-bar clamps are better for framing.

21 Compass Use it to scribe circles or transfer measurements from one object to another.

22 Drills Newer electric drills are compact, well balanced, and lightweight, making them easy and reliable to use. Today's models also offer more torque than their predecessors of the same size. Starter drills usually have a ¼-inch chuck. One with a keyless chuck will save you time and trouble when switching bits. Cordless drills free you up to move around more and you can sometimes use the same recharging pack to power up other tools.

23 Files Buy one round file, one half-round file, and one flat or mill file.

24 Glue gun Glue guns bond a variety of items quickly and easily, without mixing or clamping. From repairing bathroom tiles to creating crafts projects, a glue gun is a must-have.

25 Hammers For general nailing, purchase a 16-ounce hammer. For smaller jobs, choose a 5-ounce hammer. Sink nails with a nail set.

26 Handsaw For quick cuts, a 15- to 18-inch handsaw does the trick. Also, consider a saw with a folding blade for portability.

27 Jigsaw Whether your cuts need to be straight or curved, in wood, light metal, or plastic, the reciprocating motion of a jigsaw blade can do the trick. Capable of very small-radius cuts, this tool is well-suited for woodcrafting, model, and filigree work. Cordless models are useful for outdoor work.

28 Lead pencil A wide, flat carpenter's pencil won't roll away or break easily. If it does break, sharpen it with a penknife.

29 Level Select long levels for big projects and torpedo levels for smaller jobs. If you break the vial—new ones can be inserted into precision-molded slots

available on higher-quality levels.

30 Mallet Tap finished wood in place, bend sheet metal, or seat laminate or inlays with this soft-face hammer. Heads are commonly made from wood, rubber, plastic, or rawhide.

31 Nail belts A nail belt makes it easy to keep your tools within reach. Consider one made from a heavy-duty nylon fabric called Cordura. It's lighter than leather and more durable.

32 Nail set Use this to countersink finishing nails below the surface.

33 Plane A block plane is the simplest, smallest plane, ideal for smoothing rough saw cuts or the end grain of boards or shaving door edges to fit. Use a jack plane (one of several bench planes) about 14 inches long to smooth, trim, and shape wood along the grain.

34 Pliers For a basic workbench, purchase 6- or 8-inch slip-joint pliers, a needle-nose pliers, and channel-type pliers. Slip-joint pliers are hinged to adjust to a narrow or wide opening. Their curved, toothed jaws help grip small objects. Long-nose (or needlenose) pliers grip and bend wire and can get into tight places. Tongue-and-groove and channel-type pliers have slots or channels that position their parallel jaws to hold objects of varying widths. Locking pliers have a viselike grip that leaves hands free for work. Wire strippers cut away insulation without damaging the electrical wire. Some wires have plastic-coated handles for grip, but don't rely on this coating for electrical insulation.

35 Putty knife Use this handy tool for spackling and general scraping.

36 Retractable tape rule Choose a 16-foot tape rule with a ½- to ¾-inch-wide blade.

37 Safety goggles Choose polycarbonate or shatterproof plastic lenses that cover your eyes completely and meet safety standards set by the American National Standards Institute or the Occupational Safety and Health Administration.

38 Screwdrivers You should have a variety of sizes of both slotted and Phillips screwdrivers.

39 Snips Use tin snips to cut metal and more.

40 Square Determine 90-degree angles with a steel square or combination square.

41 Staple gun Cordless electric models let you work tangle-free.

42 Tape measures No job is too large or too small to measure with tapes that range from 12 to 100 feet. A locking model is essential if you work alone.

43 Utility knife Use a utility knife to score and cut wallpaper, flooring, roofing, laminate, and drywall. Look for one with a retractable, replaceable blade.

44 Wrench Choose an 8- or 9-inch adjustable wrench or a small set of combination wrenches.

EXTRA LUXURY TOOLS

45 Power ratchet wrenches If you work on your car as well as your house, you may be able to save yourself some time with a power ratchet wrench. This higher-torque tool drives (or loosens) a range of nuts and bolts.

46 Power staple guns If you've ever used a manual staple gun, you know how easy it can be to bend the staple or jam the gun or how difficult it may be to squeeze the staple gun repeatedly. Electric staple guns reduce these problems and speed up any tacking job.

47 Screwdrivers Power screwdrivers can easily drive screws into a variety of materials: plastic, drywall, metal, and masonry. Most come with accessories to drill and run nuts, too. Choose assorted sizes of slotted and Phillips screwdrivers. Also consider cordless models.

BUYING TOOLS

BONUS High-tech tools can be fun, but few can outlast a well-made hand tool. Designs for many hand tools date back thousands of years. With a little care, the hand tools you buy this year can be handed down for three or four generations.

BONUS Look for wooden handles or wood construction and a durable finish on metal parts. If you're not sure what tool to get and don't want to risk a lot of money, a set of wooden-handle screwdrivers makes a handsome addition to any shop.

GET A GRIP ON WOODWORKING CLAMPS

Woodworking clamps make a useful addition to a workbench because they help achieve a professional-looking job whenever wooden parts are glued together. Each of the many clamp options is made for a specific gluing project. Here are a few, listed in order of the distances they span.

MONEY $ MATTERS

48 RENT TOOLS

Any remodeling project goes more smoothly with the right tools. However, because you may use some of these tools only once, why not rent them?

For example, lease a reciprocating saw for demolition work. It has a long blade that can actually cut clear through a wall. Always make sure—before cutting—that no plumbing lines or electrical wires are in the way. If you don't, you may wind up with a do-it-yourself job that is much bigger than you thought it would be.

You may also want to rent a special nail gun called a flooring stapler that runs off a compressor. The staplers makes it quick and easy to snug each board tight and secure it to the subfloor.

To find a rental dealership, look in the Yellow Pages of your telephone book under "Rental Service Stores."

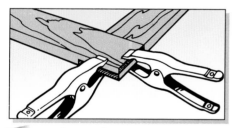

49 Spring clamps, which work like large clothespins, are good for holding thin materials, such as ¼-inch sheet goods. The clamps are available in various sizes and most have plastic tips that protect the wood surface.

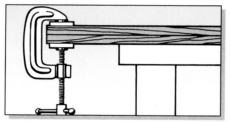

51 C-clamps work well with sheet goods and lumber. The screw allows you to apply a lot of pressure—enough to damage the material—so be sure to use scraps of wood between the jaws and the pieces you're gluing.

53 A web clamp has an adjustable fabric strap that can wrap around a variety of odd-shaped pieces, such as a wooden chair seat. Some of these clamps come with wrenches to tighten the webbing; others have built-in screws.

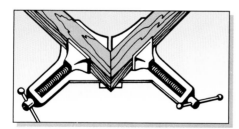

50 A miter clamp is actually a pair of clamps that forms a right angle for joining two mitered pieces of wood at exactly 90 degrees. This type of clamp is handy for gluing picture frames or mitered joints on cabinets.

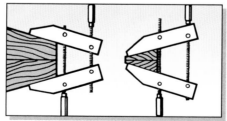

52 Handscrew clamps seldom do any damage because they are made of wood (hard maple) and distribute the clamping pressure over a large area. Their two-screw design lets you position the jaws parallel or at angles to each other.

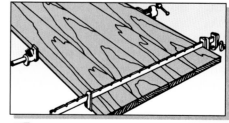

54 Bar clamps and pipe clamps span wide distances. Bar clamps have fittings attached. Pipe clamp fittings are sold without the pipe; you attach them to the length of pipe you need. Alternate the clamps as shown to keep the wood from bowing.

GREAT GADGETS FOR MINI-REPAIRS

This roundup of inexpensive home maintenance gadgets (from 50 cents to $6) will nicely fill out your basic tool collection.

58 Spackling compound and putty knife Great for filling cracks and nail holes in plaster or drywall, and dents caused by flung-open doors.

59 Wall anchors Are wobbly towel racks annoying you? Need to install some shelf standards in the garage? From toggle bolts to expansion-shield and plastic wall anchors, you'll find fasteners especially suited to drywall, hollow walls, and masonry walls.

55 Grounding adapters Here's a rescuer when you need to use a power tool or appliance with a grounded three-prong plug, and you're looking at an underground two-hole outlet. Connect the tab or pigtail on the adapter to one of the screws that holds the outlet in its metal box.

56 Double-pointed tacks No more tripping over stereo or extension cords with these U-shaped nails. Run the cords along baseboards, then tap the tacks lightly over the cords at intervals.

60 Picture hangers Give your house a personal touch with favorite paintings and framed photos. These hangers hold up to 10 pounds, yet leave only tiny holes in the wall.

57 Razor blade scraper With a retractable blade for safety, this tool does a neat job of shaving dried paint, glue, or putty off windows, floors, and tiles.

ORGANIZATION AND STORAGE

CLUTTER BUSTERS

The pride and satisfaction most do-it-yourselfers take in their projects can turn to frustration and anger when tangled cords, misplaced tools, and scattered parts interfere with their work.

Workshop clutter breeds confusion and can lead to mistakes and accidents. With a little help, your mess can turn into success.

62 Keep heavy and cumbersome materials such as paint and lumber safely out of the way in an overhead rack.

63 Hang frequently used tools on perforated hardboard. The board-and-peg system is inexpensive and adapts easily to your needs.

61 Large storage hooks keep the ladder off the floor.

64 A rolling mechanic's chest keeps small tools from mixing with other items, and provides a mobile workstation.

65 A wide variety of boxes and bins will keep small items like nuts, bolts, nails, and screws from disappearing. Storage compartments can stow under your workbench or mount on the wall.

66 EASY-REACH SANDPAPER

If you get tired of rummaging through packages of sandpaper to find the right size with the right grit, try this easy storage tip. Simply place your sandpaper in a stack on a clipboard. Then hang the clipboard from a hook at a convenient spot.

FIRE SAFETY

Because the home workshop is the storage and work area for wood products, flammable liquids, electrical power tools, and a blow torch, special precautions should be taken to keep your workshop safe.

67 Dispose of all scrap wood, sawdust, and other waste lying around on the shop floor and elsewhere.

68 Keep solvents and paints in sealed and labeled metal containers and store them in metal cabinets away from heat sources, such as your furnace.

69 Store gasoline in metal cans approved by Underwriters Laboratories (UL) and keep on hand only what you need. Keep these cans in a metal cabinet and do all refueling outdoors with a nonsparking funnel.

70 To avoid spontaneous combustion, store oily rags in an oily-waste can (sold at safety equipment stores) and empty the can daily. Or, if you don't have an oily-waste can, soak the rags in water, then dispose of them outside in a sealed metal container.

71 Inspect electrical power tools and replace any frayed cords, bad plugs, and faulty motors. Unplug and store all electrical power tools not in use.

72 Equip your shop with 20-amp electrical circuit protection to provide ample power for your tools and lighting.

73 Provide adequate ventilation in your workshop so you can rid the area of any explosive vapors or dust that might form during a project.

74 Install a smoke detector, but put it in a room next to your shop where dust isn't as likely to set it off. If you want a detector in the shop, choose one that senses heat. Test either detector often.

75 Keep a fire extinguisher handy. Make sure it is the dry chemical type with a 2-A ABC rating. This means it can extinguish electrical fires as well as fires involving combustible materials or flammable liquids.

HARDWORKING WORKSHOP

Whether your workshop is located in a newly-built addition, a basement, or a corner of the garage, organization is important if you want to use your space efficiently.

76 The often ignored space between wall studs is a handy niche for small drawer units to hold screws and nails.

77 Make sure your workbench has enough overhang to attach clamps or support a built-in vice. Fasten the back edge of the workbench to the wall for extra stability.

78 Keep bulky hand and electrical tools in a cabinet that can be locked for safety.

79 Mount exhaust fans in a window to help clear the air.

80 Have a canister vacuum handy to keep sawdust under control.

81 Use fluorescent lighting to safely brighten your work area and dispel annoying shadows.

82 Install double doors if your workshop leads to the outside

so you can easily move large materials and equipment to and from your workstation.

83 If your workshop shares space with yard equipment, a three-foot-wide doorway allows easy passage of wheelbarrows and lawn mowers.

84 Keep small items like pencils, glue, and scratch pads within easy reach with a 6-inch-deep shelf mounted just above the workbench.

85 Install drawers beneath the workbench top for storing portable power tools such as electric drills and sanders.

86 For easy power access, wire the legs of the workbench with electrical outlets.

87 Consider installing a wall phone so you can make and receive calls without leaving the shop.

BUILD IT PLUMB AND LEVEL

A surface is plumb when it is vertical and level when it is horizontal. Here's how to check:

88 To check most projects for level, simply set your carpenter's level atop the member—a shelf, for instance—and raise or lower the member until the level's bubble rests between the register marks.

89 To check most projects for plumb, hold a carpenter's level against one face of the vertical surface—a stud, for example—

and note the position of the bubble in the level. If it comes to rest between the two guide marks printed on the vial, the stud is plumb. Vertical members must be plumb in two directions, so you'll need to repeat this procedure on a surface adjacent to the one you just checked.

PROJECT PRIMER

CUTTING HOLES— TWO QUICK CARPENTER'S TRICKS

BONUS CIRCULAR SAWS

A circular saw works best when you need to cut a big rectangular opening in a large piece of plywood (or other material) without starting at the edge. Mark the area to be cut and tilt the saw so that the front of the baseplate is resting on the wood and the blade is hovering about an inch above the line to be cut. Retract the blade guard and hold it in the raised position, turn the saw on, and gently lower the spinning blade into the wood.

Once the baseplate is down flat in the wood, guide the saw forward to the end of the cut. Don't overshoot your mark, unless you're doing rough carpentry. For a cleanly cut corner, finish the last inch or so with a handsaw.

BONUS SABERSAWS

When you need to cut curves, circles, or small openings inside a piece of wood or other material, use the same basic plunge-cutting technique, only with a sabersaw. For more control, you'll need to tilt the saw so that the cutting teeth of the blade face you as you start the cut; use both hands to steady the saw during the plunge. Once you've completed the plunge, stop the saw, turn it around, and continue cutting.

A GUIDE TO SHARPENING TOOLS

90 TYPES OF SHARPENERS

Sharpening stones fall into two broad categories: synthetic and natural. Both have sharp, abrasive particles that remove tiny amounts of metal from the dull edge of a tool. Synthetic stones remove metal quicker and sharpen an edge faster than natural stones. Natural stones, on the other hand, produce smoother, sharper, more precise edges.

When you use a stone you'll also need oil to float the residue of metal fragments that the stone cuts from the tool's edge. This keeps the stone's pores from clogging, reducing its sharpening ability. It also makes it easier to draw a blade on a stone. Good sharpening oils are highly refined, nongumming mineral products.

When you're shopping for a stone, ask whether the one you're considering has been prefilled with oil. With these you only have to apply oil to the surface before each use.

Stones that aren't prefilled must be soaked in oil until they're saturated, which can take several days. Most synthetic stones are prefilled; natural stones are not.

Diamond sharpeners differ from stones somewhat. These have tiny diamond crystals bonded to a steel backing. You don't need to use oil with a diamond sharpener, and the same grit does both coarse and fine work.

91 TECHNIQUE

To sharpen a knife, place the heel of the blade diagonally across the near end of the sharpener, with the sharp edge away from you, and angle the blade at 20 to 25 degrees.

Now push the blade lightly across and along the sharpener in one sweeping motion, starting at the heel and ending at the blade tip. Stroke lightly, as if you were cutting off a sliver from the sharpener's surface. When you reach the

opposite end of the stone, flip the blade over, sharp edge toward you, and again move from heel to tip.

Periodically test the edge for sharpness by noting how easily it will slip through a piece of paper.

When you're satisfied that the blade is sharp, hone lightly to remove scratches.

92 SHARPENING ANGLES

TOOL	ANGLE
Pocketknife	15-25°
Carving knife	15-20°
Wood chisel	25-30°
Plane blade	25-30°
Drill bits	24-32°
Screwdriver	90°
Scissors and shears	80°
Draw knife	30°
Sickle and scythe	30°
Hedge hammer	28-32°
Ax	45°
Mower blade	30°
Hockey skates	90°

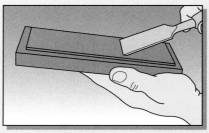

Start your collection of sharpening tools with a broad, flat sharpener. It should be at least one inch wider than the widest tool you'll be sharpening. The most popular size is 8x2 inches.

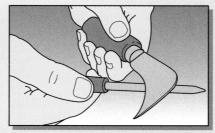

A rod sharpener comes in handy for sharpening all sorts of knives. Whet the blade diagonally up and down the sharpener, as if you were whittling thin layers from the rod. This one features diamond particles bonded to steel.

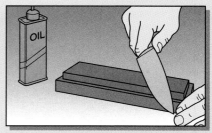

A bench stone for sharpening dull carving knives and other utensils is a necessity in the kitchen. Store it in a kitchen drawer and keep a can of sharpening oil nearby to use with the stone.

CHOOSING THE RIGHT JOINT

TYPE OF JOINT		DESCRIPTION	USES/COMMENTS
93 Butt		Two or more members joined end to end, end to face, or edge to edge.	Weak, yet good for carcass and face frame construction when pieces are glue joined.
94 Miter		Joint in which two members are cut at an angle, usually 45°, then fitted together.	Of medium strength. Preferred for molding trimwork on fine furniture cabinets.
95 Half Lap		A situation in which two members with recesses as wide as half and as deep as each is thick meet.	Strong. Excellent for face frames but requires considerable time and precision.
96 Dado		A joint formed when the end of one piece fits into the across-the-grain channel of another.	Strong and attractive. Used to support shelves in shelving units and cabinets.
97 Rabbet		Joint made when one member butts against another notched member. The notch is half the depth of the member it's cut into and as wide as the other member.	Strong. Commonly found in carcass construction, especially cabinet backs and drawers.

BONUS DRILLING OVERHEAD

Drilling overhead can produce a shower of debris. To keep you and the area clean, poke a drill bit through the bottom of a paper cup, then insert the bit into the drill. (Cut the cup down to size for a short bit.) Pull the cup back against the chuck so you can see to start the hole. Then push the cup up and finish drilling. The cup will catch the debris.

98 DIVIDE A BOARD INTO EQUAL PARTS

Divide a board into equal parts without a lot of mathematical calculations. Lay a rule diagonally across the stock, as shown. Then adjust the angle until the near edge of the board aligns with an inch mark that's divisible by the number of parts you want. The example divides the board into four equal parts. If you want three parts, you'd want the 9 on the edge.

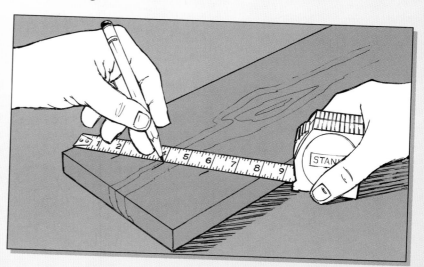

STARTING SQUARE

Whether you're building a 50-room castle, a doghouse, or just a section of fencing, there's no such measurement as *"about."* Measurements must be *exact.* Learn this now and you'll save time, money, and frustration.

Starting square, that is, with an exact 90-degree relationship between two surfaces, is the only way to make correct measurements. Most materials, however, are not square, especially ends of boards, dimension lumber, and timbers. Almost all building materials—wood, concrete, metal, plastic—have a factory milled edge, which is used for squaring the rest of the material. Here are some techniques for keeping your projects square.

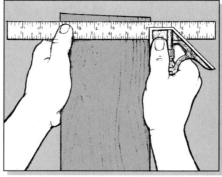

99 Check board ends for square by positioning a combination square firmly against a factory edge, as shown. If the end isn't square, mark a line along the outside edge of the square's blade.

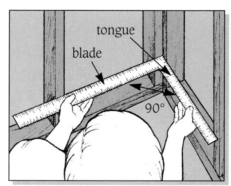

100 To determine if members that join are square, lay a framing square where the two meet, as shown. If the tongue and blade of the square rest evenly against the members, the corner is square.

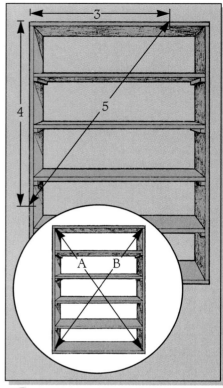

101 No framing square handy? Then lay out two sides of a 3-4-5 triangle at a test corner, *above.* The top measures 3 feet; the side 4 feet. If the corner is square, the diagonal joining the sides will measure 5 feet.

102 Check for square by measuring diagonally between opposite corners. Your layout is square if both measurements are the same and opposite sides of the rectangle are the same length.

BONUS KEEP NAILS FROM SPLITTING WOOD

To keep nails from splitting wood, blunt the pointed nail end with a gentle tap from your hammer.

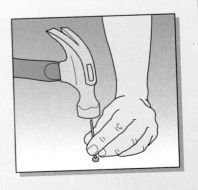

103 HOW TO CUT GLASS

By learning to cut glass (but not safety glass), you can take on a number of projects or repairs yourself and save money. You'll need a good straightedge and a general-purpose glass cutter. A standard cutter with a steel wheel is usually adequate for do-it-yourselfers.

You'll be taking advantage of the glass' inherent brittleness by scoring it with the steel wheel. Most professional glass cutters place the handle between the first and second fingers, using the index finger to guide and apply pressure to the top side; the thumb supports the underside. Hold the cutter almost perpendicularly to the glass, with the top of the handle leaning only slightly in the direction of the cut.

Before making the cut, clean the glass with a liquid cleaner, if needed. Then follow these steps:

■ Place the glass on a flat, padded surface. Several layers of newspapers, a piece of felt, or scrap of indoor-outdoor carpet will work fine.

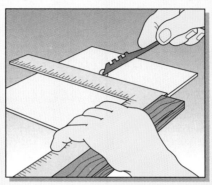

■ Lay a metal straightedge, yardstick, or piece of hardwood along your cutting line. If you use a yardstick or piece of wood, dampen its underside to prevent slippage. For curved cuts, draw the pattern on paper and put it under the glass.

■ Gently press the cutter into the glass, starting in from the edge farthest from you, and draw the cutter toward you using consistent pressure and speed. Optimum speed is 12 inches or more per second. Practice on scrap pieces until you get the right feel and timing. Always run the cutter off the bottom edge at the end of the cut.

■ Make just *one* pass over the score line. Only through practice will you learn the right amount of pressure; too little pressure and the glass will not break evenly; too much and the glass will chip or flake on each side of the line, resulting in a rough edge.

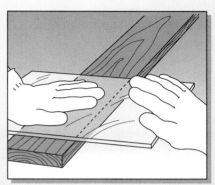

■ Tap the underside of the cut line with your cutter handle, then grip the glass on the edge closest to you on each side of the score line, thumbs on top. Snap the glass by applying downward pressure with your thumbs. Always wear gloves when breaking glass. Be careful of the sharp edges. You may prefer to put a dowel or small board (as shown) directly under the score line while pressing down on each side.

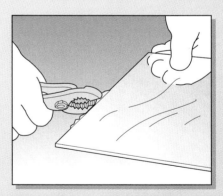

■ Use the breaker notches on the glass cutter or pliers to clean ragged edges or to snap narrow strips. For optimum wear, the cutting wheel should always be lubricated with a mixture of 50 percent kerosene and 50 percent light oil.

SIMPLE FURNITURE REPAIRS

Wobbly wooden furniture can be irritating, but fixing those loose rungs and broken joints isn't a major job.

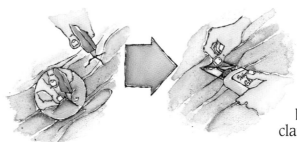

104 Tightening a loose rung

Remove the rung from the hole; take care not to loosen other joints. Scrape the hole clean. If the rung is too small, wrap cheesecloth around the end, saturating the fabric with glue.

Let glue dry. Test-fit the rung; sand the cheesecloth repair until the rung fits snugly. Apply glue and push the rung into place. Use a strap clamp or a length of rope to hold the rung in place. If using a rope, wrap it around the legs in double strands and insert a stick, tourniquet-style, to tighten the rope. Wipe off any excess glue.

105 Regluing loose veneer

On edges, gently pry up the loose veneer using a putty knife. Holding the veneer up, apply a thin coat of yellow carpenter's glue to the surfaces, using a cotton swab. In the middle of a surface, cut through the bubbled veneer using a thin-blade knife, cutting with the grain. Make a second cut at a right angle. Carefully pry up each flap and scrape off dried-on glue. Blow away residue. Work some glue under the flaps, then press in place. For both types of repairs,

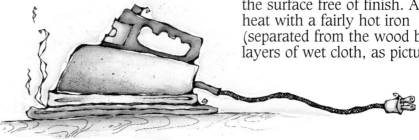

wipe off any excess glue with a damp rag. Lay a piece of wax paper over the area; weight with a stack of books or clamp with blocks of wood and C-clamps.

106 Repairing broken joints

Mend broken legs, stretchers, or rungs with dowels if the break is clean and the sections fit together neatly. First, clamp broken parts together without gluing. At an angle, drill holes for dowels through both sections. Glue the broken parts together using carpenter's glue. Insert dowels and tap them into place using a mallet. Clamp until the glue dries.

107 Repairing dents in solid wood

Steam heat may raise a dent in solid wood, but you will need to refinish the surface after applying steam. Scrape or sand the surface free of finish. Apply heat with a fairly hot iron (separated from the wood by layers of wet cloth, as pictured).

BONUS DRILLING AT AN ANGLE

If you think drilling straight is tricky, try drilling at an angle. A jig simplifies things. To make one, cut the edge of a lumber scrap to the desired angle of the hole. C-clamp the scrap of your material so it aligns with the tip of the bit on the center mark. Guide the bit into the material, keeping it in contact with the guide's edge.

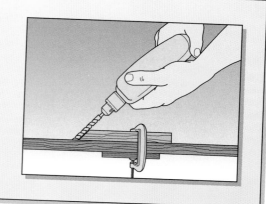

REMOVING STUBBORN SCREWS

Removing old screws can be a real headache, especially if the screws have rusted in the material, become "frozen" through corrosion, or were stripped when they were driven. With work, though, you often can back them out.

Approach a stubborn screw with care. First, test it with a screwdriver tip that fits the slot perfectly. If you encounter a lot of resistance when you try to back out the screw, stop. Otherwise, you may damage the screw slot so it can't be used at all. Try the other removal techniques illustrated here.

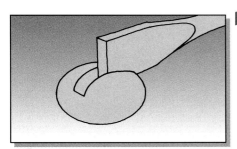

108 Remove paint, grease, or dirt from the screw slot. You can usually do this by sliding the screwdriver tip sideways in the slot.

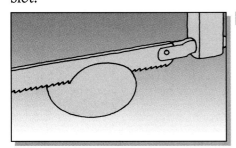

109 If the slot is too narrow to accept the screwdriver tip, you may be able to widen and deepen it with a hacksaw.

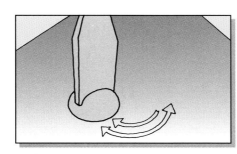

110 Turn the screw in a quarter turn. Then work it back and forth with the screwdriver. This may be enough to break the screw free.

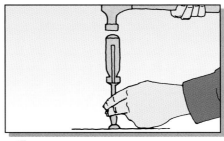

111 Firmly tap the handle of an old screwdriver in the slot; the shock may loosen the screw. Make sure you hit the screwdriver square.

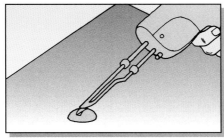

112 Heat applied to a screwhead with the tip of a soldering iron will sometimes break it free. Test the screw often.

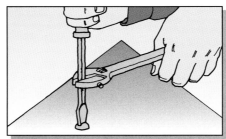

113 For extra leverage, use a square-shank screwdriver and wrench combination. Don't do this with round-shank drivers.

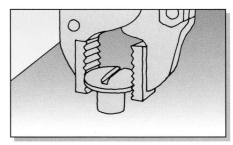

114 Once a screw is out a few turns, you can grip it with lock-joint pliers. Pliers will damage the screwhead, but they'll do the job.

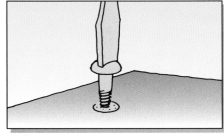

115 Don't replace the same screw in the same hole. Go to a longer or thicker screw. Or, drill out the hole and fill it with a dowel plug.

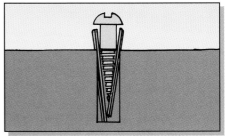

116 If you want to use the hole and screw again, fill the hole with wooden matchsticks or toothpicks so screw threads have new wood to bite. Or, tamp in a pinch of steel wool.

23

117 FREEING UP NUTS AND BOLTS

Occasionally when you tackle a repair job, you find you're stopped before you can begin because of the hard-to-budge nuts and bolts. Here are several techniques for loosening them up.

Your first thought may be to use force, but that can cause costly damage to parts. Be especially careful if you're working on antique machinery or delicate equipment.

You will need these helpers to get the job done: a can of penetrating oil, an adjustable wrench or pipe wrench (not pliers), and a small propane torch. If slotted bolts are the problem, you'll also need a screwdriver to hold them.

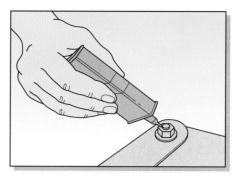

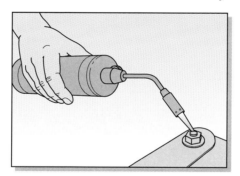

First apply a small amount of penetrating oil around the nut and to the threads of the bolt. Then adjust the nozzle of the torch to produce a fine-pointed flame and direct the flame briefly

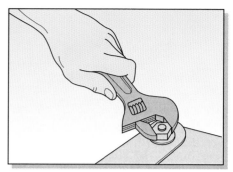

at the nut. The heat will melt the paint and break up rust and corrosion while the hot oil expands the nut and seeps between the threads of the nut and the bolt, making removal easy. A moderate amount of twisting will usually free up the nut or bolt, but more stubborn parts may require additional applications of oil and heat.

118 HAMMERING NAILS

Eliminate that all-thumbs feeling when you drive small brads and tiny nails. Use an everyday pocket comb to hold those little fasteners in place while you hammer.

Or, use a thin magnet to hold the nail upright and keep your fingers away.

Needlenose pliers can do the trick, too.

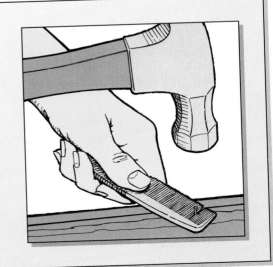

119 COMMON MILLWORK LUMBER SIZES

Thickness	Actual	Pine	Uses
⅝" material	(½" or ⁷⁄₁₆")	(same)	Drawer sides and backs
1" material	(²⁵⁄₃₂")	(same)	Cabinet facings, base frames, shelving, cabinet ledgers
1¼" material	(1¹⁄₁₆")	(1⁵⁄₃₂")	Shelving, shelf supports, furniture parts
1½" material	(1⁵⁄₁₆")	(1¹³⁄₃₂")	Shelving, shelf supports, furniture parts
2" material	(1¾")	(1¹³⁄₁₆")	Shelving supports, furniture parts, mantels

120 POPULAR LUMBER SPECIES

Species	Characteristics
Ash (white)	Broad grain patterns, strong, easy to bend, easy to work, tends to split
Birch	Finishes well, can be made to resemble more expensive woods
Genuine Mahogany	Works and finishes well, relatively easy to work
Philippine Mahogany (red lauan)	Easy to work, coarse texture, finishes well
Maple (hard)	Most adaptable of all hardwoods, takes stain and works well
Oak (red & white)	Strong, heavy, finishes well, difficult to shape
Pine	Finishes well, easy to work
Poplar	Moderately easy to work, finishes well, fairly weak, doesn't hold nails well
Walnut	Strong, durable, works and finishes well, fine grain

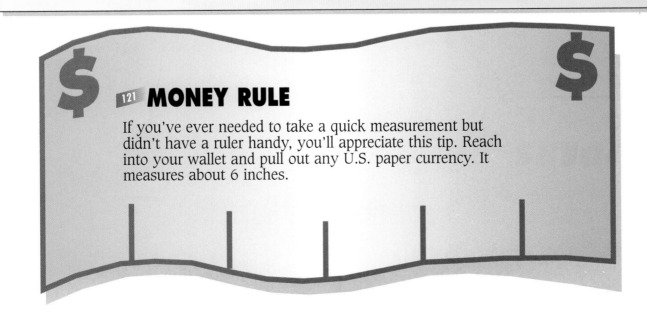

121 MONEY RULE

If you've ever needed to take a quick measurement but didn't have a ruler handy, you'll appreciate this tip. Reach into your wallet and pull out any U.S. paper currency. It measures about 6 inches.

EASY CURES FOR MAINTENANCE PROBLEMS

Excess moisture can cause costly damage to your floorboards, studs, walls, joists, and window frames. A few simple steps can save your house and your peace of mind. Here's a look at how to avoid some common moisture problems.

122 An exhausting problem Kitchen and bathroom exhaust fans that are vented into the attic rather than outdoors can cause serious damage in a matter of months. Moisture from the fans may be captured in the insulation where it can ruin drywall and even rot wood studs and joists. Clothes dryers that are vented indoors add enough moisture to the air to crumble spray-flocked ceilings, warp paneling, and cause other damage that can be expensive to repair.

123 Insulate yourself Be sure your insulation is free of gaps and holes to avoid cold spots that lead to condensation and heat leaks that cause ice dams. Replace any insulation removed when doing electrical or other repairs because even small gaps invite trouble. When installing insulation, use multiple layers with foil-faced foam on the warm side for the best protection.

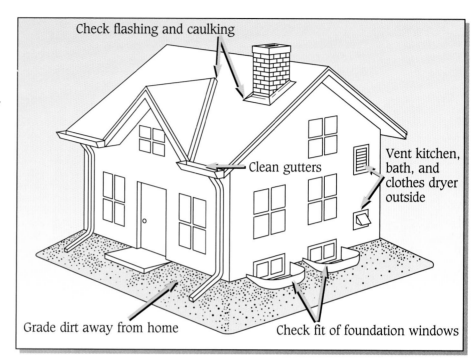

Check flashing and caulking

Clean gutters

Vent kitchen, bath, and clothes dryer outside

Grade dirt away from home

Check fit of foundation windows

124 Some basement basics A wet basement can lead to moisture problems throughout the house. Often, the key to solving a basement water problem is as simple as ensuring adequate grading at the base of the foundation, keeping gutters clean, and checking the tightness of foundation windows.

125 Proper vapor barriers Incorrectly installed vapor barriers can lead to serious moisture damage throughout a home's walls and ceilings. To keep moisture out of wall and ceiling cavities, vapor barriers must be placed on the warm side of the insulation. This means on the inside of insulation in cold climates and on the outside in warm climates. Use foil-faced foam board with taped joints on either side if you live in an intermediate climate.

126 A common sense approach Some common sense measures will minimize moisture problems. For instance, don't store cords of green firewood indoors and avoid using humidifiers in energy-efficient homes. Keep your home's flashing and caulking in tip-top condition. If you live in a cold region, use a system to keep ice from pushing up under the roof shingles and rotting the sheathing.

PORCH FIX-UP

From the porticoes of ancient temples to today's decks, porches remain the preferred spot to relax. But keeping them in shape is hard work. Here are a few tips for diagnosing and fixing a diseased porch.

127 Public enemy No. 1 is rot. The first things that go are decking and post bases. Anything that is not ventilated from the underside and doesn't get some sun will rot.

128 The porch roof is the next problem. Watch for worn-out shingles, flashing, and improper drainage. Make sure the roof is pitched to shed water and pay close attention to guttering and thin metal flashing at the roof's edge. Check the edge for areas where water can seep underneath.

129 Porch eaters include termites, powder-post beetles, and carpenter ants. Call an exterminator to eradicate all three critters.

130 As insidious as boring bugs is dry rot. A fungus spread by spores, dry rot can inundate a house before it's noticed. Once started, dry rot is difficult to stop. Replacing all or part of the porch often is the only answer.

131 As for repairs in general, it's best to defer restoring any decorative details until the porch structure is fixed. Do it in stages. Concentrate first on retaining the deck, footings, and roof. Look for parts at salvage shops or specialty milling firms. If you can't find replicas, try to preserve the "image" by choosing replacements that complement the period design.

132 Don't give up on your porch and lop it off. A porch is a vital part of your home. Removing it would be like cutting off your fingers.

DETERMINING YOUR LOT LINES

There's a fine line between you and your neighbors—your lot line. It's the legal perimeter of your property. It's also the border against which any additions to your property must be measured to meet subdivision covenants and local ordinances.

133 When it comes to lot lines, revise your vocabulary and replace the word *about* with *exactly*. You wouldn't buy a piece of property priced at "about" $100,000. But every day, buyers complete real estate transactions without knowing exactly how much property they are getting. Your real estate agent probably showed you "about" where the lot lines are, but until you know where to find the survey pins (usually yellow caps or rods buried by a surveyor), you won't know where a fence should begin or landscaping end.

134 Defining the lines yourself

There are several ways to find your property lines. The easiest way is to visit your county recorder's office or your city engineering office and ask to see the plat map of your property. If there is enough detail on the map, you may be able to locate the survey pins on the property. At least you'll know the property measurements, which should help you find the pins.

If your home is in a new development, the developer or the contractor may have a detailed plan you can copy. Unfortunately, unless you can locate your survey pins you're still guessing.

135 Hiring a surveyor

Anytime you purchase property in which you plan to invest time and money, conduct a survey. A survey and formal analysis may cost $200 to $1,250, depending on the lot size; it can cost $200 to $350 if a city lot has already been platted.

Tell the surveyor exactly what you want. You might save money if you need information about only one side of your property.

Hiring a surveyor safeguards you if your improvements are challenged by a neighbor, the city, or your neighborhood association. Then you'll have proof of working within the proper boundaries of your property.

FIXIN' UP THE FLUE

Your old chimney may appear solid on the outside while it's crumbling on the inside—putting your home and family at risk of fire.

136 If your masonry chimney is more than 10 years old, it's probably due for an inspection. Some old chimneys aren't lined and the mortar used between bricks or stones can break down from exposure to heat, smoke, gasses, and emissions from the wood you burn or from your appliances. Even the clay liners used in masonry chimneys can crack and fall apart over time. Any of these factors can lead to a dangerous and extremely destructive chimney fire.

137 Looking for trouble
Cracks on the outside indicate chimney deterioration, but troubles more commonly hide inside. Watch for falling bits of mortar, brick, and sand when you open the damper. Use a powerful flashlight to peer inside from above or below, and push on the mortar with a knife to see if it gives. Better yet, call in a professional. A chimney sweep or local fireplace or wood-burning stove dealer can give a prognosis; some even use special video cameras on fiberglass rods to get the whole picture.

138 Lining up a new liner
An ailing chimney needs a new liner, perhaps one made of lightweight insulating concrete that a professional pours into place from above. Another option is a stainless steel liner.

REMODELER'S NOTEBOOK

WHAT TO DO WHEN YOUR HOUSE SETTLES

139 As your house settles into middle age, signs of wear and tear are bound to appear. Two of the warning signs are cracking plaster or drywall around the windows and doors and an annoying tilt to the floors. It's important to inspect the damage and repair it as it occurs so your home will have a chance to age gracefully.

140 Variations in temperature, humidity, and ground moisture cause wood and other building materials to expand and contract. These changes cause old and new houses to settle.

Wood shrinkage is another factor in settling. Most new houses are built of green, moist wood. As the wood loses its original moisture content it shrinks, causing cracking in plaster or drywall.

141 When you repair cracks from settling or wood shrinkage, it's important that the joints remain flexible. Use fiberglass fabric tape and a special adhesive to hold it in place. The patch will have much more give than

spackling paste. However, you also can use nylon mesh tape embedded in and covered with drywall joint compound.

142 If your house settles enough to cause the floors to tilt, consider hiring a professional to check the foundation. House jacks are used to lift the sagging portion up to the proper level.

143 Two kinds of jacks are available. The screw jack is safest, but since it's raised with a metal pipe up to ten feet long, a screw jack can be difficult to use in tight places. The other device is a hydraulic jack. Because the hydraulic seal can break, this jack is generally used only for the lifting. To be safe, a screw jack is then put in its place to hold the house.

144 A house should be jacked up only about a quarter inch a day. The expansion and contraction of the house during the day and night will allow plaster, drywall, doors, and windows to readjust without producing large cracks.

REPAIRING CRACKS IN BRICK WALLS

145 Although masonry structures promise permanence, even the best-built ones require occasional repairs. Wait for the settling or frost action that caused the cracks to stop before beginning repair work. This may be as long as a year after the first sign of cracking appears.

146 To determine if movement is still occurring, bridge the crack with a piece of tape and check it occasionally for twists, a tear, or looseness.

1. With a heavy hammer and a cape chisel, remove old mortar from the cracked joint to a depth of ¾ to 1 inch. Wear safety goggles and heavy gloves for protection. If the joint

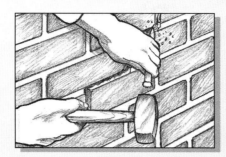

crumbles easily all the way through the wall, you should tear down the whole section and relay the bricks with new mortar. Tuck-pointing by itself will not add strength to weak masonry joints.

2. Use the point of the chisel or the tip of a mason's trowel to scrape away any remaining patches of mortar, then dust the opening with a whisk broom.

3. Wash away any remaining debris with a strong jet of water. Wetting the surface has another advantage—it improves the bond between masonry and mortar. Let the moisture soak in, and then rewet the joint just before applying mortar.

4. Mix water and premixed mortar to a putty-like consistency. With a caulking trowel, force the fresh mortar into the cleaned joints. Fill the vertical joints, then the horizontal joints.

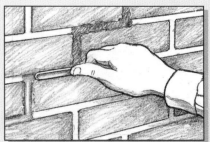

5. Now strike (form) the repaired joints so they match the shape and depth of the other joints in the wall.

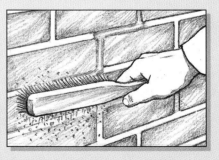

6. After striking, give the mortar time to set up somewhat. Then, use a stove brush to remove excess mortar that squeezed out from the joints during the striking operation. Within 24 hours, scrub the mortar stains from the masonry units.

STORING GARDEN HOSE

Try this shortcut to coiling a hose. Pull hose out straight to eliminate kinks, and lay in a figure 8. Then fold into a circle for storing by lifting all coils where they cross in the middle. Pull the end out of the middle and the hose uncoils freely without the usual kinking or twisting.

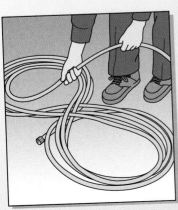

GUTTER TALK

Knowing the basic gutter and downspout components is a great way to start this do-it-yourself job.

147 Leaf-ejection systems available in molded vinyl (A), strainers placed over drop outlets (B), and gutter screens (C) work to prevent clogs in gutters and downspouts. Consider these options if you live in wooded areas where autumn leaf deposits clog gutters and interfere with drainage.

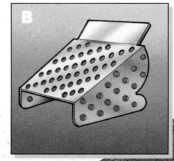

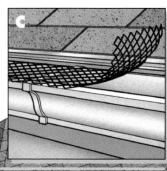

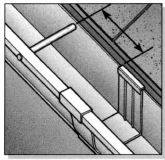

148 If possible, support gutter sections 4 to 6 sections from joints.

149 Five-inch-wide gutters suit regions with moderate or heavy rainfall. In the dry Southwest, you can get by with 4-inch-wide gutters. Slope gutters toward downspouts 1 inch for every 20 feet of run. For spans longer than 30 feet, slope from the center between downspouts.

152 Slope gutters toward downspouts 1 inch for every 20 feet of run. For spans longer than 30 feet, slope from the center between downspouts.

150 Place downspouts at corners. For gutters longer than 30 feet, install a second downspout. Small, isolated gutters also need their own downspouts.

151 Use two pipe bands for one-story downspouts, locating them near the top and bottom; for multistory homes, secure pipe bands every 8 feet.

153 Hidden fascia brackets (A) offer the cleanest look in gutter supports. Spikes and ferrules (B) allow for the fastest installation. Snap-lock brackets (C) show along a gutter's front but provide sturdy support. Straps (D) support gutters along angled fascia or where no fascia exist. Locate supports every 2 to 3 feet; center spikes and ferrules over rafter ends.

154 Heating cable on roofs and laced through gutters and downspouts prevents destructive ice buildup in heavy snowfall areas.

155 Extend gutter ends 2 inches beyond the fascia at gable ends.

156 If not present, install a continuous drip cap along the fascia at gutter locations. Fit between shingles and roofing felt. Space nails every 5 feet.

157 Splash blocks (A), hinged downspout extensions (B), and underground drainpipes (C) divert water from foundations, keeping basements dry.

31

LADDER SAFETY

Falls are the number one accident around the house. Don't become a statistic! When using a ladder, follow these safety tips:

158 Ideally, ladders should be equipped with nonslip safety feet and set on solid, level surfaces. If the support surface is not level, shim the foot of a ladder with a nonslip support such as a concrete block.

159 Set the ladder close to your work. If your hips go outside the ladder's side rails, you are overreaching and risking a fall.

160 When setting up a stepladder, make sure all four legs are supported and the spreaders are fully opened.

161 Lean a straight or extension ladder against a house so that the distance from the foundation to the ladder's base is about one-quarter of the ladder's height. Check to see that the tops and bottoms of both ladder rails are making firm contact.

162 When using an extension ladder, place it so the movable section is outermost and the top extends several feet above the edge of the roof or platform.

163 Raise the movable half on an extension ladder only to its safety mark.

164 Never adjust the height of an extension ladder when you are on it—climb down and raise or lower the ladder. Double-check that all locks are securely fastened over the rungs before climbing.

165 Be sure your feet and the ladder rungs are free of mud, grease, paint, sand, or anything else that might cause a slip.

166 Always face the ladder when ascending or descending, gripping the ladder firmly and placing your feet squarely on each rung. Do not turn around on the ladder or proceed as if you were on a conventional stairway.

167 Don't stand on the top of a stepladder. On straight or extension ladders, stop climbing when your shoulders are even with the top of the rails.

LADDER CARE AND STORAGE

168 Each time you use a ladder, check for loose rungs and shaky side rails. Keep ladders in working order by oiling moving parts and tightening nuts and bolts. Don't make "temporary" repairs and never use a bent metal ladder—it will be weak.

169 Store ladders in a dry, cool, ventilated area; avoid exposure to weather and heat sources.

170 Hang ladders horizontally on supports to prevent warping.

171 KNOW YOUR NUMBER

A roman numeral on a ladder's side rail indicates its strength, that is, the weight each rung can bear. Type III household-grade ladders are rated at 200 pounds; Type II commercial-grade ladders, 225 pounds; and Type I industrial-grade, 250 pounds. For security and durability at a moderate price, buy a Type II ladder.

172 Basic types include (clockwise from front center) a trestle ladder, a platform ladder, a straight ladder, an extension ladder, and a stepladder.

PROJECT PRIMER

173 REPLACING SCREENING

You install screening in much the same way an artist stretches a canvas—fasten it at one end of the frame, pull the material taut, then secure at the sides and other end.

The drawings below show how to improvise a "stretcher" with a couple of 1x2s and a pair of wood wedges. A spline-and-channel arrangement built into aluminum frames does the same thing.

When removing moldings from wood frames, begin with the middle rail and spring the molding loose with a chisel or putty knife. Always work from the center of the frame to the ends, applying pressure near the brads. If a molding breaks, you can find a reasonable facsimile at a lumberyard. Ask for screen molding.

For the mesh, let appearance and upkeep be your guides. Aluminum is inconspicuous, but is subject to staining; plastic and fiberglass won't stain, but their filaments are thicker which affects visibility; copper and bronze must be coated with spar varnish periodically to prevent staining.

STEP BY STEP

With a knife or shears, cut a screen that's slightly wider and at least a foot longer than the frame, then staple top edge.

To stretch, nail a strip of wood to the bench or floor, roll mesh over it, and nail another strip on top of the first.

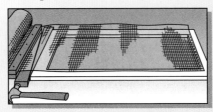

Now insert a wedge between the cleats and frame on either side. Gently tap the wedges until the screening is tight.

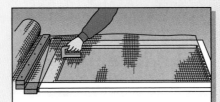

Staple screening to the bottom edge next, then to the sides. If the frame has a center rail, fasten screening to it last.

Trim off the excess, then refit the moldings with small brads. Countersink brads and fill holes with plastic wood.

To remove mesh from an aluminum frame, first pry out the spline around edges. You may need to buy new splining.

Carefully square up the frame, lay new screening over it, and cut to the same dimensions as the frame's outside measurements.

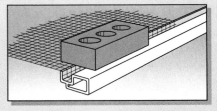

Bend the mesh's edges and force them into the channel with a putty knife. Weight with a brick to hold it in place.

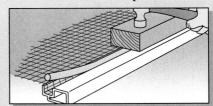

Now drive splining into the channel with a hammer and block as shown. As the spline goes in, it will pull the screening taut.

REGLAZING BROKEN WINDOWS

Fixing a broken window is an easy job you can do yourself. In addition to making you feel self-sufficient, fixing it yourself will save money. Most professionals won't take on small jobs such as windowpane replacement, and the few who do are forced to charge an exorbitant amount.

The techniques for repairing wood- and metal-framed sashes differ considerably, but neither is difficult. Here we'll take you step-by-step through the installment process. To avoid injury, be sure to wear heavy gloves whenever you work with glass panes.

174 Wood-framed windows

Tools: In addition to replacement glass (which may be purchased at some hardware stores as well as from glass

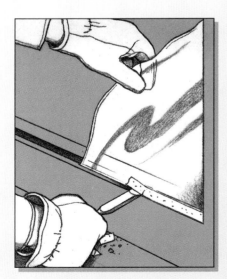

companies), you'll need push-type glazier's points, glazing compound, a glass cutter, and a framing square.

1. Start by removing any loose pieces of broken glass, then use an old wood chisel to pry up the glazing compound that holds the pane in the frame. (Soften the compound with a propane torch if necessary.) Remove the old glazier's points.

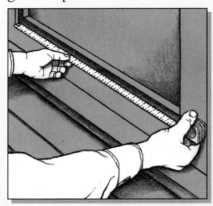

2. Determine the size of the pane you need by measuring the cleaned-out opening. Subtract $\frac{1}{16}$ inch from each dimension for glass panes and $\frac{1}{8}$ inch for acrylic panes.

3. Most glass suppliers will cut your pane for you. But if you do the job yourself, start by laying a sheet of $\frac{3}{4}$-inch plywood (larger than the piece of glass to be cut) on a workbench for a cutting surface. Make a single score along each cutoff line with the

glass cutter guided by a framing square.

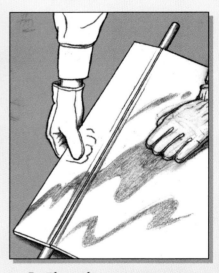

4. Place the score over a dowel or along the edge of a table and snap off the scrap piece. Trim any rough edges by snapping them off with pliers.

5. With linseed oil, prime the rabbeted area of the frame in which the pane will rest. Wait 20 minutes, then apply a $\frac{1}{16}$-inch coat of glazing compound.

6. Position the glass pane properly within the frame,

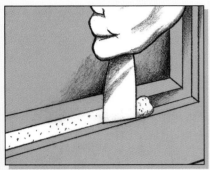

insert a few matchsticks around the perimeter to center the glass in the opening, and press the pane into the bed of glazing

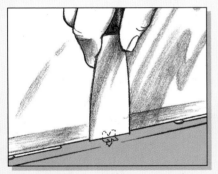

compound. Install two metal glazier's points per side using a putty knife as shown.

7. To complete the installation, roll some glazing compound into a ¼-inch "rope" and press it around the edges of the sash.

8. Bevel the compound with a putty knife held at a 30- to 40-degree angle. Allow a week

for the compound to dry, then paint around the installation,

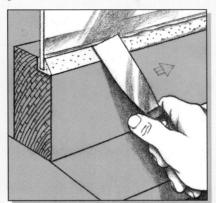

overlapping the glass about ¹⁄₁₆ inch for a tight weather seal. Don't clean the window until after the paint has thoroughly dried.

175 Metal-framed windows

Metal sashes come in a variety of configurations. Some are one-piece construction, where the glass is held in place by removable, metal spring clips (E) augmented by glazing compound or a flexible spline. Other sashes, the kind glaziers refer to as "knock-aparts," have frames that disassemble for reglazing.

With the exception of some of the one-piece spring-clip types, you should remove all metal sashes from their frames when working on them.

Like wood sashes, the one-piece steel sashes (the kind often found in basement windows) hold glass in

place with glazing compound. But underneath the sash, metal spring clips (A) take the place of glazier's points.

One-piece aluminum frames use a vinyl or rubber spline (B) which you can pry out with a screwdriver and re-install with a putty knife.

In the knock-apart category, many sliding sashes are held together with edge-driven screws at their corners (C). Once the screws are removed you simply pull the frame members away from the glass.

Some pin-type aluminum frames have internal L-brackets dimpled in place at their corners. To release them, drill out the dimples. To reassemble, make new dimples with an awl to hold the L-bracket in place (D).

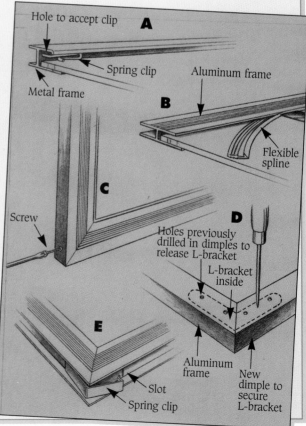

INSTALL A STORM DOOR

OUR ENVIRONMENT

176 ENERGY EFFICIENCY

In general, single-pane windows insulate at an R-1 level, double glazing rates R-2, and triple glazing rates R-3. Low-E glass rates R-3 to R-4. Remember to rely on blinds, curtains, and shades and plan on using overhangs and trees outside. All of these boost a window's thermal performance.

Like windows, exterior doors can be gateways to high energy bills. All it takes is unplugged cracks around the door edges that let air leak. One way to combat this energy loss is to install a storm/screen door. The job should take an experienced do-it-yourselfer about an hour.

177 Shopping for energy savings

If you're adding a door to eliminate energy leaks, make sure you buy a door that will serve this purpose. Doors should be weather-stripped and tightly sealed; look for weather stripping on both the door and the frame. The door sweep should also be double weather-stripped for a tight seal.

178 Before ordering a storm/screen door, measure the length and width of the inside of the door opening, and make sure that there is at least 1 inch of flat surface around the opening.

179 Installing the door

Most doors will arrive prehung. This makes installation easy for the do-it-yourselfer. Many doors also come with step-by-step instructions. Check to make sure the door cannot open while you're installing it.

180 To install a prehung unit, insert it into the opening. Level and plumb the door. Screw holes will be predrilled in the door. Drill through these holes into the wood door frame. Then screw the storm/screen door frame to the wood door frame. The last step is to attach the closing mechanism to the door.

SEASONAL SPRUCE-UPS

SPRING

GUTTER GROOMING

Rusting, overflowing, or leaking gutters can cause major damage to your home.

181 Start your gutter cleaning by removing leaves and debris; then flush the gutters with running water from a garden hose. If water gets trapped, use a plumber's snake to clear the blockage. Trapped mud and rotting leaves restrict drainage and create corrosive acids.

182 Leaf strainers or guards will help keep leaves from settling into your gutters, but may cause winter ice jams. Since the weight of the ice can break downspouts and gutters, check them every so often for ice buildup.

183 Remove rust spots with a wire brush and coat leaky seams with butyl or silicone caulk.

184 Reinforce or add gutter hangers where sections sag.

185 Never nail strap hangers over shingles. Instead, nail between the sheathing and bottom shingles. Seal nailheads with roofing cement.

SPRING EXAMS FOR YOUR HOUSE

186 **1. Testing for unsound paint** Apply a strip of masking tape to the painted surface. As you remove the masking tape, check to see if any paint pulls away on the tape. If the paint pulls away, it is not sound.

187 **2. Testing a gas pipe for a leak** Smear a fairly strong solution of concentrated dishwashing liquid over the connections; the soap will bubble where the gas is leaking.

188 **3. Testing where a door sticks** Close the door onto a strip of carbon paper. The carbon paper will rub onto the door at the point of contact. Then plane the door at the point of contact.

189 **4. Testing for condensation** Tape a piece of aluminum foil tightly against a dry basement wall. When the dampness problem reappears, check the foil. If the side of the foil facing the wall is wet, dampness is seeping through the wall. If the side facing the room's interior is wet, moisture is condensing from the damp air in your basement.

FALL

PREVENTING DRY ROT

190 Dry rot is a fungus that can slowly destroy your home's structural members by weakening and eventually dissolving wood fibers. An inaccessible and poorly ventilated attic or crawl space offers this growth the warm, dark, and moist environment it needs to survive. Dry rot doesn't require a lot of moisture; high humidity may be sufficient. If you live in an area where high humidity is common or where widely varying temperatures produce a lot of condensation, your house may be especially vulnerable.

191 To prevent dry rot, you need to eliminate at least one component of the warm, dark, and moist environment it requires. Adequate ventilation, for example, prevents heat accumulation in attic and crawl spaces.

Once every six months, check the following:

192 Make sure ventilation ridges and vents are unobstructed. For example, look to see that attic soffit vents aren't blocked by insulation.

193 Crawl space floors should be well drained, moisture free, and covered with 6-mil polyethylene sheeting that's in good condition.

194 On the outside of your house, watch for peeling paint concentrated along the bottoms of walls or under eaves. This could indicate a moisture problem inside the walls or attic and additional ventilation may be necessary.

195 Dirt around your house should never touch wood siding; a 6-inch space is recommended.

196 R-VALUE RULES OF THUMB

When dealing with insulation, a few rules of thumb to keep in mind are:

Mild climates	R-11 in the walls and floors R-19 in ceilings below ventilated attics
Moderate climates	R-19 in walls and floors R-30 in ceilings below ventilated attics
Cold climates	R-19 in walls and under floors R-38 to R-49 in ceilings below ventilated attics

For more specific R-value recommendations by region, call or write to the Department of Energy for its information fact sheet.

TIGHTEN UP AIR LEAKS

BONUS Leaky windows could account for as much as 35 percent of your home's heat loss this winter. Check your windows for drafts on a windy day by moving a lighted candle around the window edges. While tacked-on spring-metal weather stripping lasts the longest, self-stick foam and taped-rolled vinyl and felt are easier to install. Narrow spaces between the top and bottom sashes can be filled with interior rope caulk. One inexpensive way to reduce air infiltration through old or loose windows is to cover windows on the inside using double-stick tape and insulative shrink film.

Note: If there are only a few ways to exit your house in case of fire, your safest solution may be storm windows that can be opened quickly.

BONUS These interior weather-stripping steps generate few savings when gaps and cracks in your home's exterior are left unattended. Check around door and window frames and wherever dissimilar materials meet such as at framing and foundation. Clean out any old caulk or sealant and replace with new; check package instructions to determine which type suits your needs. Remember to wear gloves and wash up carefully afterward.

INSULATING YOUR HOME

It never pays to skimp on insulation. Whether you live up north where you pay heating bills or in the south where you pay air-conditioning bills, insulation saves money. Your local utility company, state energy office, or cooperative extension service can recommend what's best for your region.

197 If you want to insulate attic rafters to finish off unused attic space, the rafter depth will determine the batt size. If your rafters are 2x10, you should only put in 10-inch batts (giving an insulation value of about R-30). Thicker batts give more R-value, but only if they are not compressed. A 14-inch-thick batt will lose its insulation value when squashed into a 10-inch space.

198 To ensure that you get what you paid for, use a tape to gauge the depth of blown-in cellulose (shredded paper treated with fire-retardant) or a loose fill such as perlite or vermiculite. If you have batts put in, note the thickness by looking at the label. If you lay down two layers of batts, stagger the seams.

199 In some older homes, there's nothing separating the exterior siding from the interior plaster and lath. If you're opening one of these walls up to bare studs, this is the perfect time to spend the extra money for wall insulation. If you're not replacing an interior wall or exterior siding, you can still add wall insulation. A contractor can blow cellulose insulation into wall cavities either through the attic or through holes drilled in the outside walls that can leave lasting blemishes on the exterior.

200 Surprises often lurk behind plaster and siding. Between the studs may be horizontal boards called "fire blocking" that will keep blown insulation from reaching the base of the wall. Test for fire blocking by drilling a hole at the top of a wall and dropping a small weight at the end of a string down through the hole. Measure the length of the string inside the wall when the weight hits bottom and compare that length with the height of the wall. The only way to reach the entire wall where fire blocking is present is by drilling holes in the siding

every 2 feet horizontally and every 3 feet vertically. For your peace of mind, check the labels on bags of loose fill to see how many cubic feet a bag will fill. Then count the bags and compare the total with the cubic feet of empty space in your walls.

201 Foam insulation is also sprayed in through holes drilled in the outside walls. (Avoid foam that contains urea formaldehyde. The foam shrinks substantially if applied in the wrong weather conditions and fumes from the drying formaldehyde may cause eye irritation and other illnesses.) Urethane foam and HCFC foam are safe bets.

202 The only way to check the thoroughness of your retrofitted insulation job is to have an infrared scan performed after the insulation is installed. On a cold night, a technician will bring a scanner that takes pictures of your exterior walls and roof line. These images will pinpoint any wall cavities that weren't completely filled. Utility companies and firms that perform energy audits can tell you who to contact for a scan.

BONUS CAULK LIKE A PRO

Here's how to make a straight and even seal with a caulking gun. Put ½-inch-wide masking tape ⅛ inch from each side of the area to be sealed. Then run your bead of sealant along the crack. Even out the sealant with a wet finger until it's the desired shape and consistency. After you remove the tape, you'll have a professional-looking caulking job.

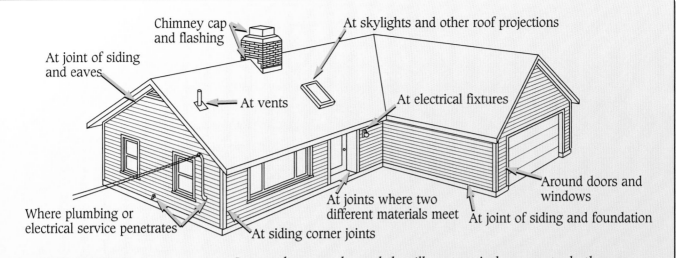

Chimney cap and flashing

At skylights and other roof projections

At joint of siding and eaves

At vents

At electrical fixtures

Where plumbing or electrical service penetrates

At joints where two different materials meet

At siding corner joints

At joint of siding and foundation

Around doors and windows

203 SEALING WITH CAULK

Different building materials swell and shrink at different rates, resulting in cracks where siding meets the foundation, for instance, or where flashing comes in contact with roofing.

Ignore these cracks and they'll widen with each passing season, admitting air, water, and insects. Your best weapon against them is a caulking gun charged with the proper sealant.

Use caulk wherever unlike materials meet. Caulk indoors, too, in basements, bathrooms, kitchens—wherever you need a water- or airtight seal. Bear in mind that no caulk lasts forever. Test old caulk by poking it with a screwdriver or nail. If it cracks, scrape it out and recaulk.

HOW TO CAULK

Take a trip down the caulk aisle in any hardware store and you're sure to be dismayed by the multitude of caulks and sealants crowding the shelves. Peek at the price tags and you'll find they can cost you a little or a lot depending on what type of job you're doing and how much sealant you need.

When in doubt

204 If you're not sure what to use, silicone caulk is always a safe choice. After all, it remains flexible and impervious to water for up to 30 years. However, because it can be expensive, you may not want to plug your whole house with it.

205 A more savvy approach is to save silicone for the small areas where you need exceptional adhesion and elasticity (such as around showers) and to buy cheaper caulks that will work just as well for other jobs.

The caulk facts

206 Acrylic latex These caulks are easy to use. When used inside, they last 3 to 10 years.

207 Butyl rubber This material is very durable for outdoor use, but application and cleanup can be difficult. The seal can last up to 10 years.

208 Siliconized acrylic These caulks are a hybrid. Like acrylic, they're easy to apply and clean up, and, like silicone, they last for 20 to 30 years.

209 Urethane foam Packaged in aerosol cans, foam expands after release, filling large and hard-to-reach gaps handily. Use around electrical outlets and new windows. The cost is high and gloves must be worn during application.

210 How-to pointers

1. Take time to master the basics before you set to work. Practice your caulking movement and pressure on a piece of aluminum foil tucked into the crevice or seam you're closing. Remove the foil when practice makes perfect.

2. Pushing a small bead before the cartridge as you caulk gives a smoother line than pulling the bead (trust us!).

3. Not all caulks are equally good at sealing cracks between unlike materials, such as wood and metal. Don't use oil-based caulks here.

4. The best bead is shallow and wide, with the caulk extending equally to the sides of the joint.

5. Have paper towels and a supply of cleanup solvent (listed on the labels) handy to help smooth the bead. The curved back of a plastic spoon makes a good disposable shaper.

ROOF REPAIR

GIVE YOUR ROOF A CHECKUP

211 To keep a roof tight, examine it every spring and fall. You needn't haul out the ladders; just scan it from all sides through a pair of binoculars, paying particular attention to the points illustrated below.

212 Ridge shingles often fail first. Look for cracks and wind damage. A leak here could show up almost anywhere in the house.

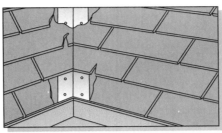

213 Valleys are another place where deterioration soon causes problems. If there's flashing here, make sure it's still sound.

214 Check all other flashings, too. They should be tight, rust-free, and sealed with pliable caulking or roofing cement.

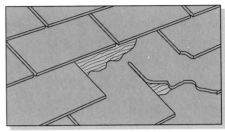

215 Any loose, curled-up, or missing shingles will admit moisture that could weaken sheathing and harm walls and ceilings below.

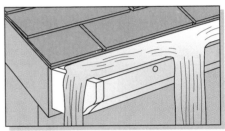

216 Wait for a heavy rain to find out if gutters and spouts are clean and free-flowing. Flooding can work up under lower single courses.

TROUBLESHOOTING ROOFING PROBLEMS

Recognize the warning signs and you can repair minor roofing problems before they turn into major ones.

BONUS Be alert for damp spots or stains in the attic, on a ceiling, on a wall, or in the basement. Drips from a leaky roof don't always fall straight down. Often, they run along rafters and down walls.

BONUS Check your exterior siding, roof edges, and fascia (the board covering the joint between the top of a wall and the projecting eaves) for water stains, crumbling, and spongy wood. The cause could be water coming through the roof or malfunctioning gutters and downspouts.

BONUS Watch for mineral deposits in your gutters. These tiny particles show roofing is getting old and worn.

REPAIR ROOF PROBLEMS

Minor problems on the roof can turn into major damage if they go unchecked. Once water gets under your shingles, it can destroy the plywood subroof, create rot in the rafters and joists, soak insulation, and ruin sections of your walls and ceilings.

217 A careful inspection twice a year almost always prevents problems before they get out of hand. Use the mild weather in spring and autumn to inspect and repair rooftop problems before the heat or cold makes it difficult or impossible.

Start any roof inspection with a careful look at what's covering the roof.

Flashing

218 Flashing is thin sheets of metal, usually galvanized aluminum, placed where shingles abut chimneys, skylights, and second-story wall sections. Flashing also spans the valley between two intersecting roof sections. A type of flashing called a drip-edge is used where the shingles end at the edges of fascia and gable ends.

219 When flashing that has been nailed in place begins to push up on the shingles, try gently hammering it back down. Put a piece of wood on top of the bulge and hammer on the wood rather than directly on the shingles. If this doesn't work or if the problem returns, there may be moisture underneath the flashing causing the wood to swell. This is a more serious problem and requires the replacement of the section that has water damage.

220 The flashing that bridges the gap between the shingles and vertical siding is held in place by the siding and rarely needs repair. Likewise for roof valley flashing. As long as this flashing is not loose or visibly damaged, it should be fine.

221 Flashing on chimneys is held in place by masonry cement or roofing tar. Over the years, the tar or cement can shrink and create gaps; repair them with tar or cement if necessary.

222 If you need to nail down any flashing, be sure to use nails made of the same type of metal as the flashing. Dissimilar metals cause corrosion.

Roof Penetrations

223 Plumbing and furnace vents are flashed with a one-piece collar, the base of which lies under the shingles. Check here for any swelling under the flashing or raised edges on the shingles and make repairs if necessary.

A Few Precautions

224 If you have an asphalt shingle roof, avoid walking on your roof after the sun has warmed the shingles. Your footfalls will loosen the tiny ceramic granules embedded in your shingles and shorten the life of your roof.

225 Also, never clean or work on your gutters from on top of the roof. Reaching down to the gutter could easily cause you to topple over. Get a ladder instead and reach up to gutters.

SHAPING UP SHABBY SHINGLES

Every day you put off repairing or replacing deteriorated shingles can mean further damage. Here's how to get the job done.

Wood shingles

226 Loose shingles should be nailed down securely. If a shingle has a minor split, slide roofing paper or sheet aluminum cut to the size of the shingle under the crack, drill pilot holes along the split, then nail along both edges. Seal the split with roofing cement.

227 Warped shingles should be split carefully at the warp with a hammer and chisel, then handled as above.

228 Moss growing on shingles can cause the wood to decay. Scrape moss off with a stiff-bristled wire brush and treat the roof with wood preservative.

229 Replace shingles that have broken edges, severe splits, or extensive decay. Remove the shingle by splitting it along the grain with a hammer and chisel, then use a hacksaw to cut out nails under the course above. Drive the new shingle into place, using a hammer and wooden block. Leave a ¼-inch space at either side of the new shingle to accommodate swelling. Finally, drive a couple of galvanized roofing nails just below the lap line for the course above and seal with roofing cement.

Asphalt shingles

230 Curled or loose shingles are the most common problem. Look for them especially after a windstorm. In areas where shingles overlap, flashing should also be checked with care. To fasten down a loose shingle, lift it gently and apply a plastic roofing cement underneath it.

231 Small cracks should be repaired with roofing cement. Trowel it into the cracks; if you make any smears, dip a cloth in solvent and wipe them up.

232 Torn or split shingles should be patched with roofing cement and secured with roofing nails.

233 To replace a badly damaged shingle, loosen nails in the shingle above by slipping a flat shovel underneath. Then pull the nails and remove the bad shingle.

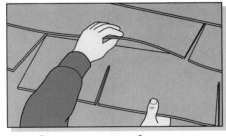

After measuring for a snug fit, cut a new piece and slip it into place under the shingle above. Align with adjacent shingles.

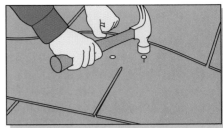

Try to drive new nails through the holes left by the old ones. If you can't, carefully seal the old openings with roofing cement.

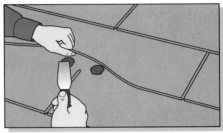

Now coat the nailheads with roofing cement, then press the upper course firmly back into place. Weight it down, if necessary.

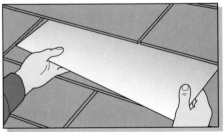

234 If you don't have any replacement shingles, you can use a piece of metal flashing to reinforce a badly damaged shingle. Cut a piece a bit smaller than the shingle, slip the metal underneath the shingle, and nail the metal to the roof. Then coat the underside of the damaged shingle with roofing cement and press the shingle back in place.

DECKS AND PATIOS

TO PAINT OR NOT TO PAINT?

235 If you want a low-maintenance deck, avoid staining or painting areas of the deck that are underfoot. Areas that people walk on always wear unevenly. You'll see a traffic pattern every time.

Instead, leave deck floors untreated and simply power-wash the deck each spring. You can use a detergent solution if the wood truly is soiled, but a vigorous spraying with plain water may be all you need to put a fresh face on your deck.

236 If you don't like run-of-the-mill, weathered decking, paint a bold design on your deck floor with colorful exterior polyurethane paint.

Start by finding a simple pattern you like. You may want to browse through a few magazines for ideas. Enlarge the pattern and transfer it to the deck floor by outlining the basic shapes with chalk. Fill in the spaces with paint. Although it will wear unevenly, it adds panache.

This deck "rug" with painted-on fringe was painted in an oversize pattern to add a sense of fun.

PRESSURE-TREATED LUMBER

An Environmental Protection Agency (EPA) review of pesticides, including the chemicals used to preserve wood, has altered the guidelines for safe use of this type of lumber. Keep the following precautions in mind.

237 Saw outside and wear a dust mask, especially if you will be exposed to frequent or prolonged contact with the sawdust from treated wood.

238 Before eating, drinking, or using tobacco, thoroughly wash areas of the skin that have come in contact with treated wood.

239 Clothes exposed to sawdust should be washed after each use. Wash separately from other laundry.

240 Use treated wood only where decay resistance and termite resistance are needed. Do not use the wood where it would come in contact with food or animal feed. Treated wood can be used indoors as long as sawdust and scraps are cleaned up.

241 Dispose of treated wood scraps by burial or regular trash collection. The wood should not be burned outdoors or in stoves or fireplaces because toxic chemicals may be produced as part of the smoke and ash.

MAKING A DECK LAST

Treating lumber does wonders to stop decay and insect damage, but attention to detail during construction and routine maintenance afterward helps the new look last.

242 Boards used for the surface of the deck should be laid "bark side down" with the semicircles of woodgrain on the ends of the board curving upward at the edges of the board. This helps the wood resist warping and cupping.

243 Fasten deck boards to joists with galvanized or stainless steel wood screws instead of nails to limit movement caused by temperature and humidity changes.

244 Pressure-treated lumber alone won't stop weather damage, so clean and waterproof your deck annually. Special applicators simplify the job.

245 Use lumber with at least a .40 retention rating where wood comes in contact with the soil.

246 When a deck adjoins one or more walls of your house, lay the joists with a slight slope to channel water away from the wall and foundation.

247 PERFECT POSTS

Here's how to set posts for your outdoor projects. Dig holes to a uniform depth or cut the posts to length after the concrete cures. For good drainage, wet the hole and pour in 2 to 3 inches of gravel. This prevents groundwater from collecting at the base of the post.

Once posts are braced in position with 2x4s, fill holes with concrete. After the concrete has set for about 20 minutes, double-check the posts for plumb and adjust if necessary. Leave the braces in place until the posts are fixed.

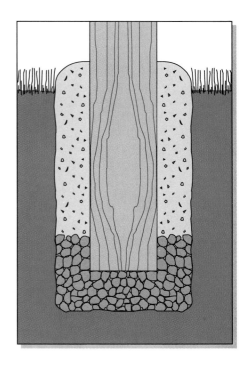

PAINTING & WALLPAPERING
EXTERIOR PAINTING: SELECTING COLORS

248 COLOR CUES

Your home's architectural style serves as one guide to choosing color. Some color and style combinations look "right" together because they have a history of collaboration.

• Pioneer homes, for example, often were left to weather naturally because paint wasn't available. That's why a saltbox style still looks at home in a neutral, weathered tone.
• Colonial houses have a long history of wearing muted shades, such as white and soft yellow.
• Victorian houses, built during a time of extravagance, are known for their exuberant use of color in flashy combinations. Popular in the late 1800s were greens, maroons, and browns.
• Contemporary houses are often painted in a few intense colors.

Pastel bands of color highlight the detailing on this Victorian-style house.

BONUS ILLUSIONS

When dealing with a simple architectural style, it's best to use a combination of two to four paint colors. To make a two-story house appear larger, you can use a light color on the first story with a complimentary light shade on all trim. A dark color on the second story will give the house the appearance of weight and solidity.

MORE COLOR CUES

249 **Roof** A pleasing contrast is important when you choose colors that go near roof shingles. But if your shingles are barely visible from the front yard, you needn't let them dictate your color choices for the rest of the house.

250 **Neighborhood** In general, your home's color scheme should harmonize, not clash, with others in your neighborhood.

251 **Number of colors** You'll probably choose a mass color for the body of the house and a trim color. But you may want to consider a third or even a fourth color for accents. Dramatize your windows and doors or accent them subtly. More than four colors often overpowers the architecture of a house.

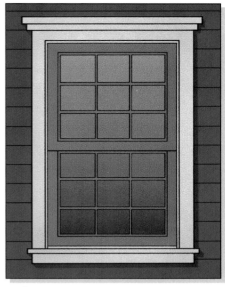

252 A sash color darker than the trim makes windows appear to recede into the facade. A sash color lighter than the frame gives the window more prominence.

COLOR PLACEMENT

253 Perk up a boxy house with colorful trim around windows and doors, along the eaves, and on the porch.

254 Unify the look of your home with subtle paint colors in the same color family.

255 Emphasize architectural detailing with a contrasting color.

256 Tie together a sprawling house by using a strong trim color all around.

257 Turn a boxy house into an eye-catcher with distinct colors that accent peaks and details.

258 Paint bold and bright colors on a large house and highlight its architectural features with white or a neutral.

259 Use a color surprise to wake up a traditional paint treatment: a bright red door on a white house.

260 Camouflage out-of-proportion or unsightly details by painting them the same color as the house.

261 BUYING QUALITY PAINT

Paints that look alike vary widely in quality. Insist on the best quality paint from a company that provides a multi-year guarantee. For exterior work, select paint that weathers well and that won't chalk as it ages. Ask your paint dealer for the "technical data sheet" on the paint your contractor proposes.

262 USING LATEX OVER OIL

Latex paint can be painted over an old coat of oil paint. Keep in mind, however, that moisture gets trapped inside the wood and tries to force its way out through the paint. The result is blistering, cracking, and peeling. Unless you eliminate the source of the problem, the new paint may fail as well. To prevent moisture problems on exterior siding from returning, eliminate the source of moisture with an interior vapor barrier.

PAINTING TREATED LUMBER

If it's color you want, most pressure-treated wood can be painted or stained. Lumber treated with preservatives weathers to a silver-gray, but adding color is a sure-fire way to perk up any deck or outdoor project.

263 Before you paint treated wood, find out what type of treatment was used. The most commonly used treatment, chromated copper arsenate (CCA), has a greenish color when new and holds paint well.

264 Other types of treatment, pentachlorophenol or creosote, bleed through paints or make it impossible for the paint to adhere to the surface. Don't attempt to paint wood treated with these chemicals.

265 CCA-treated lumber can usually be painted as soon as the lumber has dried. Most paint manufacturers recommend that you wait from a week to two months after installation depending on the weather and the species of wood. If the wood

has developed a silver-gray appearance, it's usually dry enough to paint.

266 Wood swells and shrinks. Outdoors, this wood movement can cause painted coatings to crack and peel. Painting treated wood with two coats of a high-quality latex paint is your best defense against wood movement. Oil- or alkyd-based paints are more susceptible to wood movement than latex paints which remain flexible.

267 Horizontal wood (floors, rails, and stairs) takes a beating from direct rain and sun. Even the best paints will not last long on these surfaces. On exposed horizontal wood, a semitransparent stain or oil-based penetrating stain will last much longer.

268 When staining treated wood, the green hue of the treated wood may slightly alter the colors. For more predictable results, check at your hardware store for stains specially formulated for treated wood.

CHOOSING PAINT

BONUS One of the best ways to choose between similar types and colors of paints is to compare the percentage of pigment: the higher the number, the better the paint.

BONUS With any type of paint, follow the manufacturer's directions to ensure the best result. Be especially careful to avoid applying any paint during very hot weather or in direct sunlight.

CHOOSING STAIN

269 Like paints, stains come in latex and oil-based varieties. Oil-based stains are often credited with better durability and deep penetration of the wood. They work best on porous surfaces.

270 Latex-based stains are known for color retention. They're better than oil on surfaces that are impervious to water. Latex-based stains clean up with soap and water.

271 Choose a semitransparent stain if you wish to enhance the grain or texture of the wood siding, shakes, or shingles. While this oil-based product resists bleed-through and fading, it doesn't neutralize uneven color in the wood or minimize flaws. Ask if the stain includes a preservative for woods susceptible to rot or termites. If not, you may wish to treat the wood before applying the stain.

272 Consider a heavy-bodied or opaque stain where you want to add color not available in semitransparent stains, yet still want the texture of the siding to show through. They're available in a wide variety of colors in either oil or latex base. Like paint, stains require reapplication after several years.

Painted siding

Semitransparent stain

Heavy-bodied stain

Clear sealer

BONUS **LATEX OR OIL-BASE?**

While latex and oil-base exterior paints both provide satisfactory results, there are benefits to each depending on the job.

Available in flat and glossy finishes, latex paints usually offer the best color retention. They are porous, allowing moisture to escape to prevent blistering and peeling. Beneficial to painters, latex paints are easy to apply, dry quickly to avoid bug and dirt pickup, and clean up on tools and spills with soapy water.

Oil-base paints are preferred by many homeowners. Due to their excellent hiding power, a well-done job often needs only one coat. Oil-base paint adheres to a variety of materials and performs well on chalked surfaces. It penetrates and seals wood and cracks for water-resistant results. When considering similar paints compare ingredients. Formulas with higher pigment content provide more coverage; ones with more binder offer better adhesion.

IDENTIFYING COMMON SURFACE PROBLEMS

273 Preparation is probably the least liked part of house painting but it can be the most important work you'll do. Paints and stains need a sound surface to adhere to or penetrate; without it, they won't look good or last long.

Here are some common problems associated with poor preparation, along with ways to correct the mishaps, and strategies for preventing them through proper preparation.

274 Peeling on wooden window frames/sills *(not shown):* Condensation, indicated by brown stains on the backs of paint chips, may be the source. Solution: Remove paint; caulk. Prime and paint, leaving a 1/16-inch edge of paint on the pane to prevent water from getting behind the film.

275 Alligatoring *(below):* Appearing much like the reptile's scales, this painting problem occurs when the topcoat doesn't adhere to the coat underneath. This may occur if:

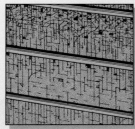

(1) the first coat of paint isn't completely dry before a second is applied; (2) a glossy coat is not sanded before repainting; (3) hard paint is put over soft primer; or (4) weather causes expansion and contraction. Solution: Remove old paint.

276 Cratering *(not shown):* Air bubbles leave depressions in the paint film. Causes include: (1) using overshaken paint before foam has settled; (2) using an unconditioned new roller cover; or (3) painting when it's too hot. Solution: Sand lightly before you repaint.

277 Blistering *(below):* Bubbles appear when paint film is applied to a wet surface. The wetness may be coming from inside or outside of the house. It also

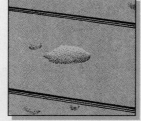

occurs when painting is done in direct sunlight or when it's too hot. Heat-absorbent dark colors are most vulnerable. Solution: If the problem is caused by moisture coming from inside the house, that problem must be corrected. Otherwise, scrape off the paint and sand.

278 Wrinkling *(above right):* Applying the paint too thickly can cause wavy crinkles. Paint should always be brushed out thoroughly. If you paint when the weather is too hot or too cold, wrinkles may result. Two problems that cause alligatoring

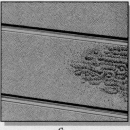

also cause wrinkling: painting a second coat before a first has dried or applying a hard finish over a soft one without priming. Solution: Sand the wrinkles or remove all the paint if needed.

279 Efflorescence on masonry *(below):* Improper preparation allows inherent salts, when brought to the surface by water, to crystallize and force the paint to peel. Solution: Remove the paint, scrub, apply a 5

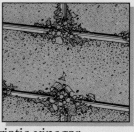

percent muriatic vinegar solution, and rinse thoroughly. An alkali-resistant primer can deter recurrence. Use a latex topcoat. If water is the constant source of damage, that problem must be solved.

280 Checking and flaking *(opposite, top):* Having lost flexibility, one layer of paint does not shrink and swell with weather changes as the other does. Too many coats of paint,

excessive paint applied at the same time (especially on rough, porous

surfaces), or application of one coat over another that's not yet dry can cause this problem. Solution: Remove all paint in extreme cases; remove and sand trouble spots in less severe cases.

281 Peeling on metal, such as gutters *(below):* Poor surface preparation is usually the villain. The lack of priming or poor priming can cause rust. Solution: Galvanized steel is

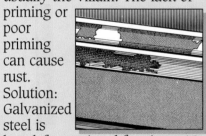

best left unpainted for six to 12 months. If the surface hasn't weathered, wash the metal with vinegar then rinse thoroughly before priming. Depending on the degree of damage, remove only the flakes or all the paint. Prime properly (some paints are self-priming).

PAINTING ALUMINUM AND VINYL SIDING

282 Aluminum siding takes paint very well, as long as you do the proper surface preparation. Before you paint, power-wash the siding or, if that's not feasible, hand-wash the siding with warm, soapy water. Rinse thoroughly. If the siding has mildewed, clean with a bleach solution, then rinse again.

283 Check closely for rough, pitted spots where the aluminum has oxidized or bare metal is exposed. Remove the oxidation with steel wool or sandpaper, and spot-prime bare metal.

284 Repaint in a color that is no darker than the original. (Darker colors collect more heat than light ones and the absorbed heat could cause the siding to warp.) For a durable finish, use a top-quality acrylic latex paint with a stain finish.

285 Vinyl siding also can be painted. The technique is the same, except that vinyl siding shouldn't be sanded, wire-brushed, or marred during the surface preparation.

286 Once you've painted siding, of course, you have to maintain the paint job regularly just as you do painted wood siding.

287 TESTING COLORS

Purchase quart cans of two or three colors you like and paint an inconspicuous spot, perhaps on the back of your house. Then, when it's dry, stand back and see what pleases your eye. Give yourself several days before making a decision and be sure to look at the colors at different times of the day—in the morning sun and the evening shade—before deciding which color you prefer.

PAINTING DOORS AND WINDOWS

288 When painting windows, work from the inside out, starting with muntins and progressing to sashes, casing, lintel, and sill. Use a high-quality sash brush to paint narrow window elements. If your hand is unsteady, use a paint shield or apply masking tape on the edges of the windowpanes.

289 As with windows, paint doors from the inside out, starting with door's recessed panels, if any. Minirollers and foam pads speed painting of narrow door elements. For tight spots around doors, use an angular sash paintbrush.

290 STAINING OVER STAIN

You can stain a new color over an old color of stain, as long as you stick with the same base as the original stain. If you're going over a solid-color stain, whether oil or latex, surface preparation is the most crucial element of the painting project to help the new finish adhere. The house should, if possible, be pressure washed. Or, scrub with a light detergent solution and hose down. After the siding is thoroughly dry, apply an alkyd primer (solvent-thinned, synthetic-resin primer) to the spots where the bare wood is showing. If you're recoating a semitransparent stain, skip the alkyd primer because the semi-transparent stain does not blister or peel—it's a penetrating coating.

291 MAKING PAINT LAST

1. Find out what you're up against first. Walk around the house, looking for problems that would interfere with—and must be fixed before—painting or staining. Look for peeling or marred paint, ripped or rotted siding, cracks in masonry, missing caulk, stained or popped nails, chalking (adhering powder), salts, mildew, wood discoloration/bleeding, rusty metal, and leaky or leaf-filled gutters.

2. Repair structural problems. Moisture, the worst villain, can take its toll on the house's interior, particularly if there are no vapor barriers.

• Paint damage that's especially bad outside the kitchen, bathroom, and laundry is a clue that moisture may be penetrating from within. Installing ducted ventilation fans in the baths or even opening windows after baths cuts down on moisture infiltration. Specially formulated interior paints that inhibit moisture from getting into walls are available. On lapped siding, you can insert wooden or metal wedges under each board where it's nailed to the stud—this allows adequate ventilation, lessening moisture buildup.

• Heavy eaves/soffit damage can be traced to poor ventilation. Add vents in the area.

• Rotted or damaged siding lets in and holds moisture which leads to a breakdown in paint film. Pack small cracks in siding and shingles with latex or butyl caulk. A badly split board may be salvageable: Coat each side of the split with waterproof glue, force the split pieces together, and secure. Replace rotted or unfixable boards.

• Fill masonry and stucco cracks with cement grout; smooth with a putty knife.

• Drive popped nailheads beneath the surface with a nail set; fill the depression with wood putty or latex caulk. If nails are rusted, sand then seal with a pigmented shellac. Sand rust on other metal using a wire brush.

• Repair breaks in gutters and downspouts and remove leaves and debris.

• Trim shrubs that touch the sides of the house.

3. If necessary, you should remove all the old paint. If the entire surface is flaking, excessively brittle, or the paint coat is thick, it's best to go back to bare wood. (If the exterior of your house has only rough spots, skip to step 4.)

• Paint-removal methods are numerous but the technique is the same—elbow grease.

• The least expensive method, and an effective one on brittle paint, is to employ both a 5-inch paint scraper and a wire brush. This method is time-consuming; however, work should be done as quickly as possible to avoid exposing bare surfaces to weather. Using a hook-blade scraper and 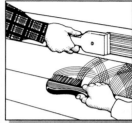 beginning in the worst spots, work the scraper underneath the paint, then lift off. Chip at the edges rather than trying to wear through unbroken surfaces. A straight paint scraper is best for hard-to-reach places. Go over the area with a wire brush.

• Another variation on this theme is the pull scraper. Hold the blade at an angle and in a single stroke, drag it across the surface. Use even, firm pressure, but be careful not to dig into the wood. When the blade gets dull, sharpen or replace it. If needed, follow up with a wire brush.

• An orbital sander removes paint quickly and (almost) effortlessly. (Use care with belt or disc sanders; they can easily mar the wood.) An inexpensive attachment for a drill is a circular wire mesh. It's used only on its side—never head-on—and handled with light, even pressure. When sanding, wear a dust mask.

• Water-soluble chemical removers are an expensive and slow means, but they minimize the need for muscle power.

Apply in small sections so you can go back and remove the paint in the recommended time. Wash the paint off; you may have to go over tough spots with repeated applications and/or a scraper. Wear gloves.

• An electric paint softener uses heat to break down the paint.  Hold the unit over the paint until it "cooks," then scrape. Sand lightly.

4. Touch up rough spots. (If you removed all paint, skip to step 5.) Touch-up jobs require less work but as much or more care, because you must make a bad and good surface uniform.

• A paint scraper works well with a wire brush, a pull scraper, or chemical remover. (If using chemical remover, be careful not to drop any on unblemished surfaces.)

• To make the surfaces even after scraping, sand the bare wood, "feathering" (lightly stroking) into the painted area about 10 inches.

5. Clean the surface by washing down the house with a mixture of trisodium phosphate (TSP) and water or a household detergent and water. Use a hose with a brush  attachment, *above.* Apply the cleaner to only part of the surface, rinse, then move on to another area. Be careful to rinse well; paint can run if put over a detergent film. After the surface dries, use a whisk broom to flick off remaining dust, especially in crannies.

• Some areas require special care. Mildew scrubs off with 1 quart of household bleach to 3 quarts of warm water; if mildew is resistant, use equal parts. *(Never mix ammonia with bleach!)*

• Chalking, a powdery residue, is a naturally occurring element in some paint ingredients. It functions as a surface cleaner when it rains. However, paint should not be applied over chalk. Thorough washing should remove it. Test by rubbing a finger over the dried area. Remove chalk with a damp cloth (if using latex) or thinner (if using oil). A wire brush aids removal on masonry. In industrial areas, you may find grayish white salts. Remove them with an abrasive cleanser such as one for sinks.

• Discoloration on uncoated ends of wood or bleeding woods can be cleaned with an oxalic acid solution. For cedar stains, use equal parts water and denatured alcohol and let dry 48 hours. For resinous knots, use turpentine or mineral spirits. Greasy spots respond to thinner or the TSP and water solution.

6. Caulk any cracks or openings where water might enter the wall and get under the paint. Replace any dried or cracked caulk. (If your wood is stripped, you should go to step 8, then come back to this step. If all wood is protected, proceed.)

• Check caulking in several places; where siding meets at the corners or at eaves, roof slopes, masonry, and foundation; around windows and doors; where plumbing or electrical services enter the house; and seams on gutters.

• Use a putty knife to remove old caulk then brush away remaining particles. Choose a caulk color that blends into the surface.

7. Protect surfaces you don't want painted. Remove or cover items such as light fixtures, house numbers, and door and window hardware. Put masking tape on glass next to window woodwork. Shrubs can be covered and be held back with rope and stakes.

8. Prime or seal bare wood, masonry, and metal surfaces. Most bare wood should be primed, including small spots that you've scraped. Exceptions include wood to which either a self-primer paint or some type of stain will be applied.

• On especially rough, unpainted masonry, apply masonry filler. Some masonry needs priming; read directions on the topcoating can.

• Some metals use self-priming topcoats. Follow application tips on the label.

292 POWER CLEANUP

Try a pressure washer for a quick way to scrub down your home's exterior—or a deck, patio, driveway, walk, or other outdoor surface. A gas- or electric-powered washer has 5 to 10 times the power of a garden hose and uses less water.

**OUR
ENVIRONMENT**

BONUS TESTING FOR LEAD PAINT

If your home was built before 1978, its exterior probably has one or more layers of lead-based paint. Lead paint may pose serious health hazards, especially to young children.

Removing lead-based paint isn't advised and it's especially important to avoid inhaling or ingesting paint particles. Call your local office of the EPA to find out how to safely remove and discard lead-based paint.

These machines include a pump, a hose that connects to an outdoor faucet, and a trigger-operated wand that pushes water through a nozzle at pressures up to 2,000 pounds per square inch. That's enough force to blast away peeling paint.

Most washers come with an alternate nozzle that delivers a wider spray at lower pressures.

Home centers sell compact pressure washers for $200 to $400. Tool rental outlets stock more powerful machines that rent for $75 to $100 a day.

293 Share rental costs with a neighbor and use the opportunity to clean off garden tools, barbecue grills, trash cans, undersides of lawn mowers, and other hard-to-scrub items.

PAINT TOOLS

Simplify painting by using the best applicator for the job. High-quality applicators hold more paint and give a smoother finish.

294 Paint pads splatter less than rollers and give a smoother finish but they don't offer quick coverage. Use them in hard-to-reach areas.

295 Rollers quickly cover large areas. Look for special rollers for corners.

296 Natural-bristle brushes work best with thin-bodied coatings such as oil-based paints, shellacs, and varnishes.

297 Synthetic-bristle brushes are stiffer and more durable than the natural ones; use them with latex paints.

298 Sponge brushes give a smooth finish but don't hold much paint.

PROJECT PRIMER

PAINTING GUTTERS

Save the life of your metal gutters with a fresh coat of paint. Here are some quick preparation and painting tips.

299 **Survey the situation.** Clean your gutters and downspouts thoroughly. Then inspect them for any problems, such as peeling paint, holes, or rust. Usually peels are the sign of improperly applied paint, a common problem on metal surfaces. Holes and heavy rust almost always are caused by standing water.

300 **Prepare and prime.** Attack rust on steel gutters, corrosion on copper gutters, and powdery white oxidation on aluminum varieties with a wire brush or steel wool. A zinc-oxide primer will help paint adhere to aluminum. When coating unpainted galvanized steel gutters, be sure to wash them with detergent or etch them with vinegar before priming.

301 **Pick the paints.** Any good quality exterior paint, oil or latex, offers excellent protection to properly prepared and primed surfaces. Special metal paints let you skip the priming stage and offer extra durability over primed surfaces. To dramatically extend the life of your gutters, consider painting the insides with an asphalt-based paint.

INTERIOR PAINTING: CHOOSING PAINT

302 Are you timid about choosing colors? You're not alone. Many people take the safe route and paint every room white. But a bold color scheme can bring a listless home to life and camouflage architectural flaws.

303 A supersaturated teal-colored wall in the living room (crisply enclosed in white trim) takes center stage, supported by the subtle interplay of white, gray, and black in the dining room. A red clock draws your eye back to the mantel. The warm tones of the wood floor hold this vibrant scheme together with a natural base.

LEARNING TO WORK WITH COLOR

304 Keep a color box. Toss in paint chips, articles, fabric swatches, anything you like. Shake it up every once in a while and see what comes to the top.

305 Experiment. Buy a quart of paint and paint a large test swatch. This shows how light and furnishings influence the color.

306 Study your problems. A too-large room will seem more intimate when painted dark. A tiny room will seem less cramped when painted in lighter shades.

307 Match the whites. All white paints have a subtle tint, either warm or cool. Coordinate this with the other colors.

308 Think combinations. Limit bold schemes to two or three colors. Pastels allow more colors within the same room.

309 Be careful with chips. Color intensity grows with wall size. A pale rose on a paint chip can look like bubble-gum pink on a wall.

TESTING A WALL COLOR

311 Color on walls reverberates and intensifies. To test a wall color, buy a quart of paint, pour the contents into another container, then let the inside of the can dry. Trust what you see on the inside of the can. That's the color you'll get.

310 Soothing is the mood of this bedroom scheme where misty hues wake you gently in the morning. The soft green ceiling color holds a hint of turquoise. On the headboard wall, lilac blue shimmers with shadings of periwinkle. Painted light gray, the ceiling beams and the wall by the door form quiet, neutral backdrops.

DISGUISE A ROOM'S FLAWS WITH PAINT

312 If walls are broken up by doorways, windows, and various nooks and crannies, paint away such interruptions with a light or white wall color applied over window and door frames and woodwork.

313 Make an unsightly feature, such as a stained brick fireplace, seemingly disappear by painting it the same color as the walls.

314 For uneven wall surfaces, a dark hue or a sponged effect hides a lot of flaws.

HOW TO SELECT PAINT COLORS

315 Wear only neutral-color clothing when looking at paint color samples.

316 Bring along any samples of items already in the room you plan to paint.

317 Take home three to five samples in your color range.

318 At home, tack up your color chips in the area where you intend to paint. It is important that you select wall color by holding the chips vertically.

319 Observe your color selections at various times of the day and evening.

320 When you have narrowed your choices to one or two, paint a small piece of wallboard as a sample and place it in the area you intend to paint.

321 Because colors look different combined with other hues, it's wise to look at your selections in proportional sample sizes. In a three-color scheme, make the largest sample the wall color, the next-size sample the color of the furnishings, and the smallest sample the accent color.

322 The larger the area you paint, the stronger the color will appear. You can counter this effect by buying a lighter value of the hue.

CEILING MAGIC

Don't overlook the "fifth wall" in your house as a powerful and surprising decorating element. It's easy to punch up your ceiling with colored paint.

323 If you put a little color on the ceilings—pale pink, pale peach, or pale blue—it gives them a little more warmth. The blues are almost like a sky.

324 Stir one cup of the paint color you use on your walls into a gallon of white ceiling paint. The ceiling will look white, but it will richly reflect the wall color.

MONEY $ MATTERS
325 CARING FOR ROLLERS

Disposable paint roller sleeves that are used once and thrown away can be neatly discarded by using a paper or plastic bag as a "mitten" to pull the sleeve from the frame. Then fold the bag over the wet sleeve for easy and clean disposal.

56

326 GETTING THE LUMPS OUT

Problem: A thorough mixing fails to remove all the lumps in your paint after it has been stored.
Solution: Using a small nail, pierce several holes in the bottom of an aluminum foil pie pan. Set the pan on top of an empty can and strain the paint through a little at a time.

327 PAINT TRAY

Before painting from a small can, set it in a larger flat container such as a metal ice cube tray. This provides a convenient place to lay your brush, and it helps prevent spilled paint on the floor.

328 EASY-OPEN PAINT CAN

For an easy-opening but airtight seal on your paint can, coat the can and lid rims with vegetable shortening after cleaning off excess paint.

329 GOOD MEASURE OF PAINT

To keep track of the amount of paint in your cans, use an oversized rubber band. Roll the band down on the outside of the paint can to match the level of paint inside.

330 WINDOW CLEANUP

Don't despair when masking tape clings to glass after the tape has been in place for a few days. Use a handheld hair dryer to warm the tape slightly. The tape should peel off cleanly.

331 CARING FOR PAINT

Here's an easy way to keep a layer of film from forming on the leftover paint stored in paint cans. After painting is complete, replace the paint can lid securely. Then store the can upside down.

332 EASY BRUSH HANGER

When you need to dry some paintbrushes, simply unravel a wire coat hanger and loop the brushes on it. This tidy, space-saving idea lets your brush bristles dry without bending or breaking.

333 SPIN-DRY PAINT ROLLERS

Here's how to fluff up your paint roller, even if it's soggy with latex or glue. First, rinse as usual. Then cut off the handle of an inexpensive roller frame, leaving enough stem to fit into a drill. Attach the wet roller, chuck the assembly into the drill, and "spin-dry" the roller inside a paper bag.

BRUSH UP ON THE BASICS

Before you set out for a paint store, consider the following:

Choosing the Right Paint

334 Buy the right paint for the right surface. For almost all interior projects, you can choose either water- or oil-based thinned paints. Neither is likely to need thinning; what matters is whether the paint cleans up with water or with a solvent. Look for cleanup directions on the can.

335 Water-based paints, also called latex paints, wipe off floors and wash out of tools with soap and water. They're fast drying, nearly odorless, and pleasant to use. They are, however, less durable than oil-based paints.

336 Oil-based or alkyd paints require cleaning with paint thinner. As a result, they're messier to use but are more durable in areas such as kitchens and bathrooms that demand hardworking surfaces. These paints dry more slowly than latex paints and give off an odor as they dry.

MONEY $ **MATTERS**

341 # HOW TO ESTIMATE PAINT COSTS

Check the paint label; it usually states the one-coat coverage you can expect from 1 gallon of primer or paint. With that information, here are the measurements and calculations you will need to make.

Measure the perimeter of the room (all walls) and multiply the result by the ceiling height to get the square footage. Round off to the full foot. Don't deduct for windows or other openings unless they add up to more than 100 square feet.

Divide that figure by the number of square feet a gallon of paint promises to cover. Double the quantity if you're planning two coats. Round up the number and buy as close to it as possible to eliminate unnecessary waste.

Priming the Surface

337 In a new house, all the surfaces need a coat of primer to seal surfaces and provide "tooth" to hold the new paint. Also apply a primer if you're painting a raw surface; making a significant change in color, such as from dark to light or light to dark; or if you are covering a glossy surface with a latex paint or latex with oil-based paint.

338 The primer you need depends on the kind of paint you use. Read the label or consult your paint dealer.

How Much Shine Do You Want?

Latex and oil-based paints come in three types of finishes: flat, semigloss, and high gloss. Besides the difference in appearance, the finish

determines how well the paint will wear and, as a result, where you should use it.

339 Flat paints generally work well on interior walls and ceilings. As a rule, they offer easier, better coverage than other finishes and cost less. The duller the surface, however, the less resistant it is to wear.

Although flat finishes tolerate moderate abuse, they do not stand up to repeated scrubbings as well as semigloss and high gloss paints.

340 Semigloss and high gloss paints protect doors, windows, and other woodwork. These paints are also good for walls subject to especially hard wear such as in kitchens and baths, because dirt washes off easily.

SELECTING THE BEST TOOL FOR THE JOB

With the right applicator you can have a picture-perfect paint job. Just match the tool to the project.

Unlike some products in which there are few discernible differences, painting tools can provide either labor-saving design or laborious work. Purchasing a less-expensive tool may cost you later in extra effort. Each type—brush, roller, and pad—has an effective use and limitations. Opt for the most comfortable one that gives the type of finish you want.

One tool not shown here is the airless spray applicator. Once only for professionals, it's been scaled down to the needs and price of homeowners. Make sure you get the correct nozzle size for the job (some are adjustable).

Brushes

There's a brush for every purpose—and some you haven't even thought of. For a professional-looking job, the bristles must be compatible with the paint or stain you use. Here are the choices:

342 Natural bristles (the best are made from hog's hair) are designed for oil-based paints, varnishes, and shellacs. They go limp or splay outward when used with latex.

343 Nylon bristles are ideal for oil, but they also can be used for latex. Nylon is more durable.

344 Polyester bristles are compatible with any paint or finish. Because these bristles retain both stiffness and resiliency, use polyester when working in high temperatures or use a brush with a nylon/polyester blend for both durability and resiliency.

345 **Pads**
Designed first for shakes and shingles, pads are good on smooth surfaces. They apply paint faster than a brush, come in many sizes and contours, and can be cleaned or replaced. Close fibers are the key to pads that can hold a lot of paint and apply it smoothly. The more fibers, the better. Trim guides allow cutting in close without marring adjacent surfaces.

346 **Rollers**
Best on flat surfaces, rollers are known for fast application, yet they can spatter. The surface texture you're covering dictates cover nap length; the smoother the surface the shorter the nap. (Packages describe correct uses.) Although a lamb's wool roller cover holds more paint, it costs more (though it's not thrown away) and isn't as good with latex. Synthetic covers can be cleaned but are often discarded; they work with latex or oil. The best cores are plastic or phenolic-impregnated paper. Seven- and 9-inch rollers are good for walls and ceilings. Use smaller sizes for corners, moldings, and frames. Extension poles will stretch your reach.

347 Wall brush: Used for broad surfaces such as siding. Comes in 3- to 6-inch widths; 4 inches is best for a do-it-yourselfer.

348 Angular sash/trim brush: Best for getting in tight places, such as around doors, windows, and corners.

349 Flat sash/trim brush: Used for more narrow works such as sash and trim. A 2-inch width is a good choice.

PAINT PRODUCTS SHOPPING LIST

It isn't necessary to spend a fortune for painting equipment, but it pays to buy the best you can to prevent headaches in the long run.

350 Products for Surface Preparation

- ☐ Step stool or ladder
- ☐ Scraper to remove old paint
- ☐ Sanding pad and sandpaper
- ☐ Liquid deglosser (sometimes called liquid sander)
- ☐ Disposable gloves
- ☐ Detergent such as trisodium phosphate (TSP) to wash walls
- ☐ Spackling or patching compound
- ☐ Narrow-blade putty knife
- ☐ Drywall primer (for new surfaces)
- ☐ Primer/sealer with stain blocker
- ☐ Mildewcide (if needed)

351 Supplies for Applying Paint

- ☐ Masking tape
- ☐ Large drop cloth
- ☐ Good quality paint
- ☐ Screwdriver or paint can opener
- ☐ Paint-mixing sticks
- ☐ Paint tray and tray liners
- ☐ Paint roller and extension handle
- ☐ Roller cover
- ☐ Synthetic-bristle trim brush
- ☐ Edge guide
- ☐ Bristle comb

352 Extras

- ☐ Heat gun and scraper
- ☐ Disc sander
- ☐ Paint can pouring spout
- ☐ Liquid glass-masking solution
- ☐ Airless paint sprayer
- ☐ Power roller
- ☐ Premium grade roller covers
- ☐ Mini paint rollers
- ☐ Brush cleaner and conditioner

CHOOSING A QUALITY BRUSH

353 Brush bristles against the back of your hand. They should be springy and not fan out too much.

354 To hold more paint for a faster job and to ensure flexibility, bristle lengths should vary.

355 A good brush has space plugs of plastic, metal, fiber, or wood to increase its paint-holding ability and to ease cleanup. The ferrule, a metal strip, should be rust-resistant.

356 Wooden handles are best if unpainted; plastic handles should be solvent-proof.

357 A good brush has flagged, not flat, bristle tips—much like the split ends of hairs. These produce the smoothest application because they can pick up more paint, retain it, then release it more evenly. The more flagging in the bristles, the better.

REMODELER'S

PAINT LIKE A PRO

An unskilled handyman can slap a coat of cheap paint on the walls of a garage or basement workroom and that may be all he wants. However, it's false economy to invest $12,000 in a new master suite finished with a $200 cut-rate paint job. The flaws will bother you long after the loan has been paid off.

358 Good painters give a lot of attention to prepping a job. They should start by cleaning and degreasing the surface. All surfaces should be sanded smooth before the first coat and later between coats. Final sanding of the surface to be painted should be done with 220-grit garnet sandpaper.

359 Where there's old paint on the surface, glossy finishes should be sanded or a liquid deglosser used. Indoors or out, loose paint should be scraped off and the surface beneath primed.

360 As with many home repairs, labor makes up the major cost of painting. Generally, professional painters receive a discount from paint retailers, but don't expect the savings to be passed along. Besides, you don't want today's small savings on supplies to turn into major corrective work later.

361 For interiors, apply a latex primer. Use a washable paint on the walls (an eggshell or satin finish) and a high- or semigloss on the trim.

362 For new drywall, there are specialty primers that can equalize the surface texture differences between the paper and the joint compound. Don't try to skip a step by applying wallpaper directly to unpainted drywall. You'll be setting yourself up for problems down the road when the time comes to strip off the wallpaper.

PROJECT PRIMER

363 PAINT PERFECTION FOR CABINETS AND SHELVES

Properly painted cabinets and shelves can take a beating without chipping. Here are tips to help you apply a finish that lasts.

1. Fill holes and imperfections with wood putty; let dry.

2. Use medium-grade sandpaper to smooth the entire surface of the project, including filled areas. Be sure to sand pieces that have been stained as well.

3. Use a tack rag to wipe away all sanding dust and other residue.

4. For bare wood, brush on a primer. For wood that's been previously stained or painted, brush on a primer sealer. These products prevent old finishes from seeping through the new coat of paint. Let dry.

5. Once the primer or primer sealer is dry, sand the entire surface very lightly with fine-grade sandpaper.

6. Use a tack rag to wipe away sanding dust.

7. For your final color coat, choose a high-quality alkyd paint. Alkyds, commonly known as oil-based paints, generally feature a leveling agent that smooths away brush strokes as the finish dries. You may need to apply two coats of paint to cover the old finish. The paint should cure within several days; then it's ready to stand up to heavy use.

HOW TO BRIGHTEN YOUR BASEMENT

364 When considering a basement paint job, the big question is: Will it stick? Many people hesitate to take a brush to their basement walls and floor, fearing that the paint won't adhere to the masonry. And it won't, if you have an unsolved moisture problem. Otherwise, with the right preparation and the right paint products, coating your concrete with color is a great way to give it a fresh outlook—and one that will last.

365 Prep Steps
What you do before you paint determines how long the paint will stay on. Follow these steps:
• Remove any peeling paint with a wire brush, and make all needed masonry repairs.

• Degrease the surface by scrubbing it with detergent and water.
• Neutralize the alkaline in the mortar by applying a mix of one part hydrochloric acid to three parts water. Be sure to wear rubber gloves and goggles.
• Rinse everything with water.

366 Brushing Up
Several types of paint will adhere to masonry. Tough-wearing epoxy paint is the top pick for floors and walls that are washed frequently. Cement paint also works well, unless the walls have been painted with another type of finish. Latex paint, the easiest to apply, adheres to foundation walls that are in good shape.

Check with your local paint supplier or hardware dealer to learn what's best for your walls. Apply the paint with a stiff, short-bristle brush or a roller with a long nap.

367 CEILING FAN PROTECTOR

If you need to paint the ceiling but have a ceiling fan, relax. You don't have to go to the trouble of taking the fan blades off. Instead, cover them with the plastic bags that protect your newspapers. They're a perfect fit and protect the blades from paint drips.

368 PAINTING OVER WALLPAPER

It's okay to paint over wallpaper if conditions are right. First, the wall covering should be tight to the wall with smooth seams. If a few peeling edges are the only problem, you can scrape off the loose area with a razor blade, fill slightly recessed spots with a bit of spackling compound, then sand. If your wall covering has any sheen, first wipe it with mineral spirits to remove the filmy topcoat. Then, prime the area with an enamel undercoat that has a stain killer. Now you're ready to paint. (Keep in mind that flat paint hides imperfections better than glossy.) If the covering is old or dull, it's likely made of paper, in which case you simply prime and paint.

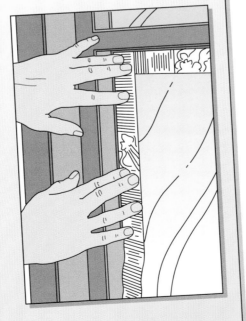

BONUS NO-MESS WINDOWS

To paint around window panes easily and quickly, use newspaper strips instead of masking tape. Cut the newspaper into 1½- to 2-inch strips, dampen in a small dish of water, squeeze out the excess water, and apply to the panes where they meet the wood. The dampened paper sticks just long enough to allow you to paint. After you're finished painting around each pane, carefully peel off the strips.

PAINTING PROBLEMS SOLVED

369 QUESTION: Can a water stain on a painted plaster ceiling or wall be repainted with interior latex paint?

ANSWER: Yes it can, if the ceiling is first treated with shellac or a stain sealer made specifically for this purpose. The sealant will keep the stain from creeping through the paint.

370 QUESTION: What causes recently applied semigloss paint to peel from varnished wood trim?

ANSWER: Either the varnish was so glossy that the new paint couldn't adhere or the varnished trim was coated with wax or furniture polish. Remove the paint, then sand the varnished surface or clean it with liquid sandpaper until the varnish looks dull. Now the paint you apply won't peel.

371 APPROXIMATE PAINT DRYING TIMES

	Latex	Alkyds
To the touch	1 hour	4 hours
To handle	4 hours	6 hours
To top-coat	6 hours	overnight

* High humidity can prolong drying times.

OUR ENVIRONMENT
DISPOSAL GUIDELINES

372 The best way to get rid of paints is to simply use them up. Use your leftovers as primer coats, or give the paints to a neighbor or a community project. Paint thinners can be repeatedly strained and reused.

373 Good storage helps keep paints out of the landfill. Tightly sealed oil paints can last up to 15 years and latex up to 10 years. Paints, solvents, strippers that can no longer be used, and sludge from any paint-stripping operation should be taken to a hazardous-waste facility.

PROJECT PRIMER
374 PAINTING OLD DRYWALL

For a silky smooth finish on old drywall, ceilings or walls, follow this guide:

1. Scrape off texture and loose paint with a 6-inch putty knife.

2. Don't remove popped nails. Instead, drive a second nail directly beside it so that the new nail head secures the existing nail in place. Dimple the drywall with a hammer.

3. Using a 6-inch drywall knife, fill all holes and dimples with drywall compound. Tape and mend all cracks and open joints. Let compound dry.

4. Apply a thin layer, or skim coat, of drywall compound across the entire ceiling or wall surface using a 12-inch drywall knife. Let dry.

5. Lightly sand surface with 100-grit sandpaper. Touch up surface with compound as needed. Let dry.

6. Sand surface with 120-grit sandpaper.

7. Using a roller with a ¼-inch-thick nap, apply latex paint to the wall or ceiling surface. Let dry.

8. Lightly sand entire surface and touch up imperfections with drywall compound. Let dry.

9. Cover surface with one to two coats of paint as desired.

PAINTING FLOORS

375 PAINTED FLOOR BASICS

With a steady hand, masking tape, stencils—and patience!—you can create artful checks, stripes, or hearts. Mask off simple squares or stripes or use ready-made stencils for other shapes. With a bit more skill and artistry, you can design and cut your own stencils. Intricate patterns, however, are best left to professionals.

1. Prepare the Floor. Remove any old wax then sand the area. If you sand to the bare wood, seal with a coat of thinned oil-based primer.

2. Paint the Base Coats. Use two or three coats of oil-based paint in the color and finish (flat paint or shiny deck enamel) of your choice.

3. Create Your Designs. Practice on scrap wood before attempting the real thing. Brush paint (usually oil-based, but acrylic paint is okay) between masked lines, or dab paint through stencils.

4. Protect Your Handiwork. Wait for 24 hours, then protect your design with at least three coats of low-luster or shiny polyurethane varnish. Let the floor dry 24 hours between each coat.

376 PAINT A GAME BOARD

You can paint the game board (below) on a floor in your house. Using masking tape as a guide, paint the areas and seal them with two or more coats of polyurethane. Fill small bags with beans or rice and use them as game pieces. Kids, even adults, will spend hours at play.

This scuffed pine floor features a painted-on, oversize game board ideal for playing Parcheesi, hopscotch, backgammon—even checkers and chess.

Are painted floors practical in high-traffic places? You bet! Painted on a plywood floor several years ago, this traditional diamond design still looks great. The vintage motif makes a perfect background for homey antiques and casual gatherings with friends.

INTERIOR PAINTING:
SPECIALTY TECHNIQUES

377 RAG PAINTING

Almost any type of cloth is suitable for rag-rolling—cotton sheeting, cheesecloth, chamois, lace netting, terry, or burlap—but the type of cloth you use will affect the look. Make sure you have an ample supply of cloth. A 12x14-foot room will require the equivalent of a double bed sheet.

Select Your Technique

Simply dab a freshly painted surface with a wadded piece of cloth, or roll the crinkled fabric across the paint, changing directions frequently to create an irregular design. Because the resulting markings are quite pronounced, most designers prefer pastel shades over a neutral ground. The main rule of thumb is that the background color should be several shades lighter than the paint you rag-roll. Use gloss or semigloss paint, which will not be absorbed by the wall—or by the rag—as well as flat paint.

How-To Help

To begin, spread paint over a larger section of wall, using a roller or a brush. While the paint is wet, dab or roll the cloth across the wall, changing directions frequently as you move across the wet surface. Cover the entire painted area, making sure that no brush strokes or roller marks remain. Complete the entire ragging process before the paint dries. You may want to enlist the help of a friend.

DESIGN IDEA

378 STRIPE IT RICH

It takes more creativity than cash to dramatize a boxy room with paint. To stripe your walls, brush on a cream base, then use a level to draw lines 15 inches apart. Fill in alternate sections with taupe for a contemporary covering that soothes with its simplicity.

The owners of this boxy 13x13-foot room got a sophisticated, serene look with a few gallons of paint and a minor reshuffling of furniture.

Paint dabbled with rags over a base coat produces the elegant look of crumpled fabric. The effect varies depending on the type of rag you use and the way you wield it.

379 COMBING

Combing is one of the simplest decorative paint finishes to learn. As with any painting project, the first step is to purchase the right materials at an art store, paint shop, or hardware store.

- **Base paint** The base is usually a satin finish, enamel paint.
- **Oil glaze** This transparent product, sold under a variety of brand names, gives a luster to finishes. Although glazes come pretinted, you can mix your own for more color choices.
- **Colors** The best colors to mix with the oil glaze are artist's oil colors. Because both glaze and paint are oil-based, the mix will be slow drying and easier to manipulate.
- **Tools** You can buy a plastic comb made especially for the combing process, or make your own by notching a piece of stiff cardboard, pressed board, or even a rubber-edged dustpan.

How To Create Special Effects

The type of special effects you can create with combs and colored glazes are limited only by the imagination. Textural zigzags, swirls, waves, stripes, and checkerboards require just a few basic steps:

Step One: Apply the base coat over the entire area you want to cover.

Step Two: Mix the glaze with the oil colors and apply to an entire wall.

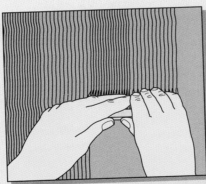

Step Three: Starting at the ceiling line, pull the comb down through the glaze using long strokes and even pressure *(above)*. You'll have to work fast, allowing the glaze to dry only about 10 minutes before

you drag a comb through it. Get someone to help you with this step or use a large comb to cover the surface more quickly. Be sure to wipe the glaze off the comb after each stroke to prevent buildup. Don't worry about keeping a steady hand or applying even pressure; irregularities create an appealing textural quality.

Step Four: To layer colors or designs, as in the checkerboard pattern *(below)*, simply comb a second coat of glaze over the top. The last coat will be more dominant, so you'll need to determine which color and design you'll want to stand out.

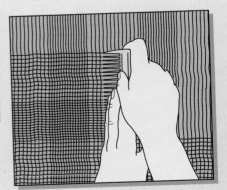

380 GLAZING

Flat paint stops the eye. A glazed wall brings in another color and gives it a parchment effect so that you look through the outer layer of paint and beyond it.

To glaze your walls, paint on a base coat, let it dry, then mix up a batch of glaze using this recipe:

☐ 1 part interior oil-based paint
☐ 1 part glazing liquid
☐ 2 parts paint thinner

Apply the mixture to a 4-foot-wide section of wall, making big W's with a roller. For this first step you will be leaving about two-thirds of the wall surface uncoated with the glaze.

Next, saturate a cheesecloth (one that has been prewashed and dried) with the glazing mixture. Rub the saturated cloth over the 4-foot section of glazed wall as if you were mopping a floor; this spreads the glaze.

Then, take a second piece of clean, dry cheesecloth and blot the excess glaze leaving a soft, mottled finish. Use a dry, round-tip brush to blot at the ceiling line and into corners.

As you work remaining sections of the wall, continually check for and blot drips with clean, dry cheesecloth.

To give walls a glow of color, brush an ochre glaze over the wall, then soften it with a second glaze of raspberry.

381 GIVE WALLS THE LOOK OF AGED PLASTER

To give walls the aged look of plaster, as in the photo *below,* try this technique:

• Purchase matte-finish, water-based paint in cream, taupe, and gold.

• Paint the walls with a base coat of cream. Thin taupe and gold paints half-and-half with acrylic matte medium. Colors stay vibrant if you thin paint with acrylic matte medium (available at art-supply stores). When used to thin interior paints, it lends depth and sheen to the finished product.

• To apply the thinned taupe and gold paints to the walls, use rags and brushes. A little paint goes a long way. Working in 4x4-foot sections, alternate patting and dabbing the paints on the wall.

• Use a soft touch and run the paint out to the edges. Don't worry if you don't like the way it looks. You can go right over it again. If it's too dark, bring in the light color.

• To complete the finish, create a border using taupe paint, a spray-on granite-look paint, and cream paint. Mask off the ceiling and create a level line along the walls. (The border in the photo *below* measures 5 inches deep and includes the molding at the ceiling edge.) Then paint the border with taupe paint. After the paint dries, spray on a light coat of the granite-look paint. (Protect walls and ceiling from spray.) Complete the look by painting thin feathery lines randomly across the border. Detailing takes a couple of hours.

382 If the plaster finish on your walls is rough and broken, enhance the look with a painted finish that mimics the look of old plaster. Apply a sponged and ragged finish with three shades of paint. The finish will be best if you apply paint with wet rags and sponges, and try to duplicate the look of smoke. Edge a broken section of plaster with pencil lead or create veins with pencil lines.

LINGO

Before you choose a wallcovering, master the vocabulary. You'll be so glad you did when you're leafing through sample books.

383 Washable versus scrubbable coverings
There is a substantial difference between washable and scrubbable. If a wallcovering is washable, you can wipe soil from the surface with a damp cloth and maybe a little mild soap. If a covering is scrubbable, you can go after stains with vigor, time after time, without damaging the surface.

384 Strippable wallcoverings Strippable coverings have adhesives and strong facing materials that allow them to be peeled off the wall without steaming, wetting, or scraping. However, you cannot rehang the covering once you have stripped it.

385 Prepasted wallcoverings A boon to do-it-yourselfers, prepasted goods eliminate most of the mess that used to accompany hanging wallcoverings. The back of each roll is coated with dry glue; you just dip the roll in water and apply it.

386 Wallcovering squares
An old idea whose time has come again, these 12x12-inch modules simplify hanging. They are especially handy for small areas, such as kitchens, baths, and closets. Each square contains a complete design motif, eliminating the chance of mismatching patterns.

387 Pretrimmed wall-coverings At one time all wallcoverings came with white borders called selvages. These protected the pattern during shipping and handling, but it took a steady hand to trim them off during installation. Now, with the exception of a few costly hand prints, nearly all wallcoverings come from the manufacturer pretrimmed.

388 PREPARING WALLS

Remove old wallcoverings. Repair blemishes in the walls. Using sandpaper, roughen old gloss or semigloss oil-based paints. Seal with latex sizing. On new plaster or drywall, wait a month before papering, then paint the walls to seal them. Paint or finish woodwork before you hang the paper.

389 TOOLS

Wallpaper tools are available separately or in kits. In addition to a pasting table (two or three card tables or two sawhorses and a sheet of plywood will do), ladder, and drop cloth, you will need a razor knife and plenty of sharp blades; a wide (6- to 10-inch) putty knife; a pasting brush or roller (for prepasted wall coverings, get a water tray and sponge instead of the pasting brush); a smoothing brush; a seam roller; a yardstick; scissors; a large sponge; and a plumb bob to mark vertical lines.

390 USE PUSHPINS

When hanging your own wallcoverings—especially the heavier and wider ones—use several pushpins to secure each strip near the ceiling while you smooth the paper downward. Remove the pins, then smooth and cut the excess paper at the ceiling.

HANGING BORDERS

391 When hanging a prepasted border on a wall covering, do not wet the border. Instead, use a vinyl-over-vinyl adhesive.

392 Let a wallcovering dry for 48 hours before mounting a border on top of it.

393 Don't just wet and hang a prepasted border. To activate the adhesive, borders must soak for the amount of time specified in the directions, and then they must sit for a few minutes before hanging.

394 For easier handling, fold a wet prepasted border accordion style (without creasing), making sure the adhesive never touches the front. Have a partner hold the folded end while you position small sections.

395 After positioning the border, use a sponge to smooth out wrinkles and help the border adhere.

INSIDE THE SHELL
WALLS

396 CRAFTING THE LOOK OF STUCCO

A stucco finish adds texture to any room. It's easy to apply, too. Begin with a clean, dry wall. Working from top to bottom on a 3-foot-wide area, lay on a $\frac{1}{8}$- to $\frac{1}{4}$-inch layer of drywall compound using a cement trowel to skim the compound flat against the wall. At the same time, pull the trowel away from the wall while spreading the compound to create a rough texture. Repeat the spreading and pulling action until the surface is irregularly roughened. Clean the trowel and use it to sweep broadly across the roughened areas to create high and low texture; use a side-to-side and up-and-down motion. Continue to the next 3-foot-wide section, blending the areas. Complete before the drywall compound dries.

397 WET PLASTER SCREWS

Before putting a screw in drywall or plaster, wet it first. The water will set the plaster and help the screw hold better.

398 CHIPPING OLD BRICK

If you live in an old house with plaster covering brick walls, consider exposing the beauty of the "party" brick. Use chisels to chip away the plaster surface, then wash the walls with $\frac{1}{4}$ cup liquid Tide (without additives or bleach) diluted in 1 gallon of lukewarm water. The brick is soft, so be careful when using a steel brush. Then seal the bricks to preserve them and enhance their beauty. Sure Klean Brick Depth, manufactured by ProSoCo, Inc., was used in the kitchen pictured *right*.

REMODELER'S NOTEBOOK

DRYWALL JUST LIKE A PRO

Unless the job is small, most contractors farm out their drywall work to subcontractors. No matter who does the job, the drywall should be "glued and screwed"—never nailed—to studs, rafters, or trusses. A construction adhesive bonds the drywall to the wood framing. This strengthens the wall and makes the drywall flexible. Insist on $\frac{5}{8}$-inch drywall on ceilings and $\frac{1}{2}$-inch on walls. On ceilings, $\frac{1}{2}$- and $\frac{3}{8}$-inch drywall can sag.

BONUS Tape and cover with joint compound. When the compound is dry, make sure it is properly sanded by the drywaller. A contract clause may be in order here, requiring that "walls be sanded smooth with 220-grit paper and made ready for painting." Otherwise you'll end up paying extra for your painter to do this.

BONUS In high-moisture environments such as bathrooms, don't let your contractor use conventional or even greenboard drywall as backing for tile. Even the types of drywall marketed as being waterproof can be destabilized by water over long periods causing your tile to peel off. Be sure your contractor uses an approved backer board such as Wonder-Board, Durock, or Dens-Shield. For the highest quality job, tile should be set in "mud," an inch-thick layer of concrete troweled over wire mesh to provide a substrate for tile.

399 COMMON SENSE WALLBOARD REPAIRS

When the wall that needs repair is made of wallboard rather than plaster, here's what you need to do. Damaged areas can be cut out to the nearest stud. Nail a piece of scrap lumber—called a nailer—to the stud so that you have something to attach to. Headers can be nailed or screwed at the top and bottom of the hole so that half of the width supports the old material and half supports the new at the point of the horizontal joint.

PATCHING A SMALL HOLE IN WALLBOARD

1. Make the hole rectangular or square.
2. Cut a filler patch, to which the final patch will be fastened. This should be a piece of wallboard or lightweight wood bigger than the hole, a size that will fit through the hole diagonally.
3. Put a screw in the center of the patch to use as a handle.
4. Apply white glue to the front surface of the patch, around the edges only.
5. Slide the patch into the hole; you may have to do a little cutting to get it to fit.
6. Use the handle to pull the patch toward you tight against the back of the existing wallboard until the glue dries. If the patch is very heavy, fasten it to the old wallboard with four screws.
7. Cut the final patch. Measure carefully, because this plug should fit the hole exactly.
8. Cover the back of the plug with glue, insert it into the hole against the filler patch and secure it with joint tape and joint compound.

LOAD-BEARING, OR NOT?

Before removing a wall in your home, determine whether it's load-bearing. Have an architect or engineer make the final determination.

400 You can spot a major structural beam or joist in your house by looking for several 2x boards spiked together side by side with no joints lined up. Also, the height of a structural beam would never be less than 8 inches.

401 To determine whether a wall is load-bearing, go to the basement (if you have one) and look carefully at the layout of beams and rafters. Does the wall you're considering razing rest on a major joist or beam? If it does, it is almost certainly a bearing wall. If the wall is positioned in the living space above without regard to the location of the bearing joists or beams supporting the first floor, then it is most likely a partition wall.

402 If your house rests on a slab or if you plan to renovate the second floor, the same inspection technique described above applies except that the joists and beams will be in the overhead space.

FINDING STUDS IN WALLS

Studs are the vertical members in a wall, usually 2x4s. Wallboard or plaster and lath are nailed into the 1½-inch stud edge. Anything hung from a wall will be secure if you fasten it to a stud underneath.

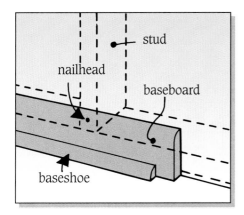

403 To locate a reference stud, look for an electrical outlet box. Electrical boxes are nailed to the stud, usually on the right side of the stud. Thump on the wall next to the box; the wall will sound solid, not hollow, over the stud. Once you know the location of one stud, you can measure 16 inches to find the next one. The only exceptions to the 16-inch rule occur near corners and in narrow rooms where ceiling joists may lie on 24-inch centers.

404 A magnetic stud finder is actually a nail finder. If your walls are covered with drywall or plaster and wooden lath, magnetic stud finders should do the trick; walls finished with plaster and metal lath will give you a false reading.

405 Electronic density-sensitive stud finders are the most accurate. Instead of reacting to nails, this finder readers the relative density of a wall indicating the stud inside. Simply press a button and slide the finder along the wall. When it reads the extra density of a stud or joist, the sensor lights up. Not only will you find the stud, you'll also be given its exact center.

PROJECT PRIMER

HOW TO REPAIR WALL CRACKS IN PLASTER

Whether or not you realize it, your house fidgets on its foundation. That eventually causes hairline or larger cracks on interior plaster walls, usually running diagonally from corners, doors, or windows. Here's how to fix them.

406 FILL HAIRLINE CRACKS

Wall surface filler, such as Spackle, available in powder and paste forms makes good filler for hairline cracks.

1. Widen the crack with a screwdriver to about ⅛ inch and blow out any loose plaster. For a long-lasting repair, dig about an inch past each end.

2. Wipe the fissure with filler, pressing it in with your finger. You may need to repeat this in an hour or so.

3. Always seal patches with primer before painting; otherwise, the repair might "bleed" through the finish coat.

407 PATCH LARGE CRACKS

Patching plaster must be mixed with water but because it's stronger than wall filler, it's better for broad cracks.

1. Undercut wide cracks with a hammer and chisel to make them broader at the bottom than on the surface. This helps lock in the patching plaster.

2. Mix patching plaster in small batches, following the label directions.

3. Thoroughly wet the crack just before patching to make a good bond between old plaster and new.

4. Pack patching plaster into the crack with a wide-blade taping knife or a putty knife.

5. Wait about 24 hours. Then level off the repair with a second application after wetting the area.

6. After another 24 hours, smooth the dried patch with fine sandpaper or a damp sponge. Then seal with primer before painting.

CONCRETE HANG-UPS

The first step to anchoring anything to a concrete or masonry wall is drilling a hole and that requires a good drill equipped with a masonry bit.

408 If you have a lot of hanging to do, rent a hammer drill. These drills vibrate the bit back and forth while drilling which helps to remove the small stones in the concrete. If you drill more than four or five holes with your regular drill, you risk burning out the motor.

409 For drilling in concrete or masonry, carbide-tipped bits are a must. Anything less wears out quickly and overloads the drill. For hammer drills, special high-strength bits are required to withstand the drill's rapid fire. Most rented drills come with the proper bits. Make sure you know the exact hole size you need to drill before starting. This information is normally provided with the fastener.

410 Drilling into concrete is not a strength contest. Let the bit do the work. If you hit something that stops forward progress, pull the bit out, and examine the tip. If you see metal shavings, you've hit a section of metal reinforcing bar. Your best bet in this case is to plug the hole and drill another one. If you don't see metal shavings, you've probably hit a hard pebble. Break the pebble by tapping it with an awl, remove it, then continue.

Fasteners

411 The type of fastener is determined by the size and weight of the object you're going to hang. The most common

412 Look for these concrete fasteners in your hardware store. Clockwise from top left: hex-head masonry screw, lag screw and expansion shield, slot-head masonry screw, expansion shield and nail, plastic anchor, and wedge anchor.

fasteners are shown in the photo *above*.

Slot-head or hex-head masonry screw. These are the easiest anchors to use. The screw cuts its own threads in the concrete, but you still must drill a pilot hole. Masonry screws are somewhat expensive but well worth the price.

Lag screw and expansion shield. This anchor requires you to drill two holes of different diameters—one in the concrete for the shield and one slightly smaller hole through whatever it is you're anchoring with the screw. Aligning the two holes can be tricky.

Plastic anchor. This inexpensive, light-load anchor also requires two different-size holes and works on the same principle as the lag screw and expansion shield.

Wedge anchor. This steel device is inserted into the hole, with the threaded end out. Tightening the bolt on the threaded end mashes a loose-fitting collar on the other end against the inside of the hole until the bolt is wedged in tightly.

Expansion shield and nail. Tap this light-load anchor into the hole and then hammer the nail directly into it. The nail pushes the two wings out and snug inside the hole.

SHEET PANELING AN OLD BASEMENT

413 How much sheet paneling do you need? Divide the perimeter of the room (in feet) by the number of walls (usually four). Deduct a half panel for a door or fireplace and add a half or full panel (depending on the size) for internal walls and partitions. The result is the number of sheets you need.

414 If possible, acclimatize paneling by storing it for at least 48 hours where it will be used. This prevents warping. Stack it flat, with 2x4s as spacers.

415 To make the walls sturdy, nail 4x8 sheets of ⅜-inch drywall to the wall frames before adding the paneling. This provides a level surface for the finished wall so it will not give when leaned against. (Check your local building code. Some codes require a "fire wall" of drywall.)

416 Paneling shrinks a little after it's up, so it's a good idea to paint every joint in the drywall underneath the same color as the joints in your paneling. If the paneling does shrink later, you won't see white board behind it.

417 Before nailing up the paneling, "try it on" by placing panels against the walls of the room. Some panels look better together than others. Move them around until you're satisfied with the look.

418 To prevent splintering the face of your panel, it should be cut face up if you use a sharp crosscut saw or a plywood blade in a table saw. If you use a portable circular saw or saber saw, cut the panel with its face down.

419 Install the first panel in a corner. Check with a level to make sure it is vertically straight. Then nail 1-inch nails (colored to match the paneling) into panel grooves. Use a nail every six inches near panel edges and every 12 inches on the middle grooves.

420 DRILLING A HOLE FOR STEREO WIRES

Problem: You need to drill a hole through the floor to run wires for your stereo system, but the carpeting snags and wraps around your drill bit.

Solution: Make a small slit in the carpeting with a utility knife and insert a short piece of copper tubing over the spot where you want to drill. The tubing will shield the bit and protect the pile of the carpeting while you drill.

PINING FOR WOOD

421 To care for pine wood floors, use a wood soap sometimes, other times use a little ammonia in water. Damp-mop as needed. For gouges, lightly sand the spot, restain it, and brush on polyurethane.

422 To install pine floors, purchase No. 3 grade or better of 1x8 pine boards. (Watch out! No. 1 grade can cost 10 times more than No. 3 or No. 2 boards.) Consider using pine car siding (also called shiplap); many people prefer the look and it often arrives from the lumber mill in a drier state. If you do buy car siding, install it wrong side up so the V-groove faces the subfloor.

423 Buy 20 percent more pine than you think you will need because there's bound to be some waste with less-expensive grades. You'll want knots and some imperfections for their charm but deep gouges and other more serious marks become waste.

424 Once you make your purchase, bring the boards into your house and leave them for three weeks to dry and adjust to your home's climate.

SILENCING FLOOR AND STAIR SQUEAKS

Every house has at least one: a floorboard or stair tread that groans and creaks every time it's stepped on—and always the loudest when you go to make a midnight raid on the refrigerator. When you stop to consider the weight and traffic borne by floors and stairs, it's not surprising that they may occasionally develop problems needing attention.

425 Anatomy of a Floor

In the flooring, the 2x8-, 10-, or 12-inch joists stretch from exterior wall to exterior wall. Bridging (use of diagonal or solid supports between joists) stiffens the joists and keeps them from twisting. The subfloor (planks laid diagonally or 4x8 plywood) adds still more rigidity. Building paper quiets floors by separating the subfloor and the underlayment or the finish floor. The underlayment (¼-inch plywood) strengthens floors and provides a smooth base for the finish floor.

The primary problem comes from changes in humidity which cause these various wood members to swell and shrink at different rates and results in squeaks when the boards rub against each other or the nails.

426 Anatomy of a Staircase

Your home's staircase has many parts, all of them interlocked with sophisticated joinery that's usually concealed.

A pair of stringers (boards) stretch from one level to the next. They support a series of steps called treads.

Complications arise when risers are added to fill the gaps between treads. Finally, there's the balustrade, consisting of the handrail, balusters, and a newel post.

Most stairway squeaks are from a tread rubbing against the top or bottom of a riser or a stringer.

Whether the wood stress causing the problem is in the flooring or the stairs, quieting these annoying squeaks is mainly a matter of locating them, then securing boards or stair components that have loosened and are rubbing against each other. If you're lucky, you'll have access to these trouble spots from below. If not, there are ways to handle them from above.

427 Silencing Floors from Above

1. With hardwood floors, drill angled pilot holes wherever needed; then drive spiral-shanked flooring nails into the

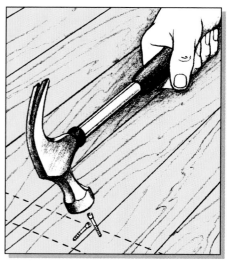

subflooring. Set the nailheads and fill the recesses with color-matched wood putty.

2. For carpeted floors, pull back the carpeting and pad, then drive ring-shank nails into the floor joists beneath the squeaky floor.

428 Silencing Floors from Below

3. Enlist a helper to walk on the finished floor above while you look for movement of the floor joists and of the subfloor from below. When you find the problem area, first check to make sure that diagonal bridging between your floor joists (if any is nearby) is firm. Making the bridging more snug may do the trick.

If the noise comes from between the joists, drive a tight-fitting piece of solid bridging up between the joists until it makes contact with the subfloor then end-nail it in place.

4. To silence a subfloor that has worked away from the joists, drive glue-coated shims into the gaps between the sub-floor and the joists.

429 Silencing Stairs from Above

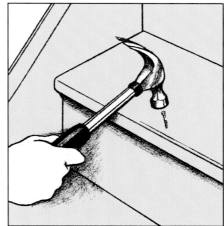

5. To fasten down the front edges of a tread, drive spiral-shanked flooring nails at an angle into predrilled holes as shown. (It's useful to have a helper stand on the tread as you nail.) Next, set the nails and conceal the hole with wood putty.

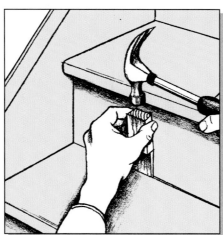

To eliminate squeaks at the back edge of a tread, drive one or more wedges of scrap wood (coated with glue) into the gap between tread and risers. Later, trim away the protruding wood.

430 Silencing Stairs from Below

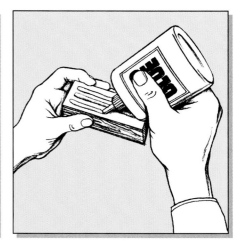

6. Squeaky stair treads that have parted company with their risers respond well to treatments from below.

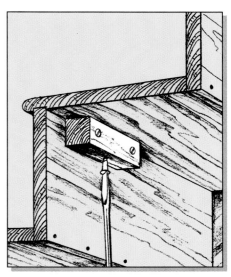

Drill pilot holes through the small blocks of 2x2s for the wood screws that will attach to both the tread and the riser. Then coat the contracting surfaces of the blocks with wood glue and drive the screws in both directions.

HARDWOOD FLOOR FIX-UP

Here are some tips for keeping your wood floor looking as good as new:

431 Remove superficial blemishes with fine steel wool and a good floor cleaner. If water spots persist, sand with fine sandpaper. Follow with steel wool dampened by mineral spirits.

432 To remove tougher stains, rub the area with steel wool and mineral spirits then rinse with vinegar. If the stain remains, sand.

433 If the stain still hasn't come out, try one or two applications of oxalic acid, a powerful powder bleach. Wear rubber gloves when working with oxalic acid and follow mixing directions closely. Rub the mixture into the stain a little at a time and allow the floor to dry between applications.

434 Sand out cigarette burns that aren't too deep. Follow the sanding with steel wool dampened with soapy water. When finished, wipe with a soft cloth. Refinish when dry.

435 Tips for Refinishing the Treated Area

Sand off the wax from an inch or two of the surrounding surface or use a commercial cleaner to remove wax buildup. Then rub steel wool over the entire area to roughen it.

Stain the sanded area to match your floor. First, however, try out various colors on scrap wood of the same type as your floor.

Apply a finish coat. Use surface sealant for a small area, or for an entire room, you may want to use one of the new penetrating sealants.

(Penetrating finishes should not be applied to wood floors that have been previously coated with varnish or polyurethane.)

Apply the new sealant evenly; let dry and apply another coat. After the last coat is dry, apply a coat of wax.

REMODELER'S NOTEBOOK

FLOORING UNDERLAYMENT: HIRING A PRO

436 Whether you're going to install wood, tile, or sheet vinyl flooring, your contractor will have to prepare the floor to receive the finish flooring. Insist on a premium subfloor of tongue-and-groove plywood, glued and screwed to the framing.

437 The subfloor should be covered with a rated underlayment that has been face-sanded to provide a perfectly flat, stable supporting surface for the finished flooring *below*. The contractor should not apply premium floors over a plywood subfloor containing open knotholes. Make sure the underlayment is grade-stamped as such, and that its face has been fully sanded, not plugged and touch-sanded.

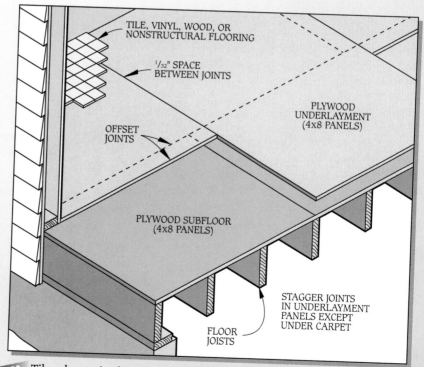

TILE, VINYL, WOOD, OR NONSTRUCTURAL FLOORING

$1/32$" SPACE BETWEEN JOINTS

OFFSET JOINTS

PLYWOOD UNDERLAYMENT (4x8 PANELS)

PLYWOOD SUBFLOOR (4x8 PANELS)

STAGGER JOINTS IN UNDERLAYMENT PANELS EXCEPT UNDER CARPET

FLOOR JOISTS

438 Tile, sheet vinyl, and wood flooring require underlayment installed on top of a quality subfloor. A grade stamp on plywood will show whether it can be used as underlayment. If underlayment is not installed or is installed incorrectly, seams in the subfloor will transmit through the finished flooring.

439 PAVER TILE TIP

As a floor covering, Mexican paver tile is durable, easy to maintain, and fairly inexpensive. Because the tiles are very porous, protect the surface with a penetrating sealer before installation. A good way to do it is to spread a plastic sheet on your lawn, lay out about 150 tiles at a time, and spray the finish on the tiles using a clean bug sprayer. After each batch dries, stack the tiles and repeat the process until all the tiles are sealed.

440 PRICING TILE

Besides its stunning good looks, ceramic tile has many other advantages. It's easy to maintain, tough to harm, and available in a wide selection of shapes and colors.

Glazed ceramic tiles typically sell for $2.50 to $8 per square foot. Quarry tile is in the $3 to $5 range. Installation varies by locale; a typical price is $3 per square foot. If your subfloor needs work to accommodate tile, the installation price may be higher. Unconventional shapes and numerous corners add to the installation costs.

441 Ceramic tile makes a beautiful, low-maintenance kitchen floor. It has drawbacks, however: tile isn't as for-giving as wood and vinyl, and you can say goodbye to glassware that falls off the countertop.

REMODELER'S NOTEBOOK
RESTORING WOOD FLOORS

442 Warped floors may require attention to the joists beneath or a simple application of weight (bricks on a sheet of scrap plywood work well) followed by careful nailing with 12d finishing nails to hold the boards in tightly against the joists.

443 Many old wood floors require refinishing—something that can pose a major restoration challenge. The obvious, but expensive and disruptive, solution is to have them professionally sanded and refinished. A quicker and less costly option is to remove darkened, built-up wax and varnish with steel wood pads dipped in denatured alcohol.

444 If the varnish is spattered with latex wall or trim paint, first slather some lanolin-base hand cleaner on the spots and let sit for 10 minutes. Then scrape off the paint with a putty knife. Pigmented wood putty should be matched to the floor and applied to nail holes and small cracks. This won't work for large cracks or gouges; you'll have to replace, sand, and refinish those.

445 That done, make sure the work area is well ventilated and that any nearby flames, sparks, or heat sources are extinguished or removed. Pour alcohol onto a 4-foot-square area of the floor. Let it work for three to five minutes. Scour it with steel wool and wipe with a clean rag. The wood grain will shine through beautifully.

DESIGN IDEA

JAZZING UP VINYL

446 To create a lightning bolt zigzag down the center of a vinyl tile floor, first measure the diagonal of your floor, then cut enough 1¼-inch-wide strips of vinyl to fit. Although some flooring manufacturers offer these narrow strips precut, you can get a one-of-a-kind look by cutting your own.

447 The process is not difficult. You can cut the tiles with a table saw or with a utility knife and a straightedge. (Tile cuts easier when it's warm.) The saw simplifies the process if you have a lot of tiles to cut, but remember that it's necessary to allow for the width of a saw blade when you're figuring cutting lines. Because a knife blade makes a narrower cut than a saw blade, it gives you less waste.

448 A table saw gives a clean, accurate cut. Just clamp a straightedge to the saw base, and hold the tile firmly against this guide. Allow for the width of the blade in measuring.

449 Not all vinyl tiles are suitable for cutting. Look for those without a bevel on the edge. As you plan your patterns, keep in mind that the saw kerf may prevent you from cutting one tile into four equal squares. Cut some tiles and then experiment with patterns. Play with the design until it suits you and your floor.

450 A diagonal checkerboard pattern on the floor will make a narrow room seem wider. To enhance the illusion (and add an element of fun), create a zigzag strip—a lightning bolt of vinyl—down the middle.

TREATING COMMON TILE FLOOR STAINS

Material	Stain	Treatment
Ceramic	**451** Soap film	Scrub with vinegar; rinse.
	452 Grease	Keep stain wet for one hour with a 1:4 lye/water solution; rinse and dry.
	453 Gum, tar, wax	Scrape off solids; treat remainder with a rag soaked in kerosene; dry.
	454 Inks, dyes	Keep stain wet with household bleach; warm-water rinse and dry.
	455 Food stains	Scrub with a trisodium phosphate solution (or bleach); rinse and dry.
	456 Paint	Soften and remove with acetone.
457 Slate, quarry tile		Blot all spills once and scrub with detergent. Spills that penetrate these porous materials become permanent. To prevent stains, apply a sealer.

458 PRICING VINYL

Prices range from $1 to $5 per square foot for do-it-yourself installation and from $2 to $6.50 per square foot for professional installation. Do-it-yourself installations may not be covered under warranties but the materials will be covered.

459 LAYING CERAMIC TILE OVER VINYL

Can ceramic tile be installed on top of vinyl flooring? You bet, as long as you have a solid, nonflexing floor structure. If your existing floor seems to give with your weight, you'll need to investigate the floor structure before laying tile. Movement in the subfloor could cause the grout and possibly the tile to crack.

However, if your vinyl flooring is well adhered to a sturdy underlayment, you can install ceramic tile right over it. Before you begin, clean the floor thoroughly to remove any floor-care products but do not sand or scar it. Install the tile using an epoxy or organic adhesive and follow the procedures recommended by your supplier.

Vinyl floors that are poorly adhered or foam-cushioned must be covered with a stable material such as ⅜-inch plywood to provide a flexproof underlayment. This will raise the height of your floor.

Do not attempt to peel off old vinyl flooring. Older vinyl floors may contain asbestos. Although these floors pose no health risk while intact, removing one could release harmful asbestos fibers. Asbestos-removal experts must use special equipment to safely remove this type of flooring.

REPLACING DAMAGED SECTIONS OF CARPETING

460 Don't try to patch-repair a section of carpeting that already shows noticeable wear: Your new-looking patch will probably stand out more than the original damage. Take care to install patches with the pile running in the same direction as the surrounding carpet.

461 With rubber-backed (or other glued-down) carpet, simply glue in your cut-to-size patch.

462 For jute-backed carpet installed with tack strips, follow these steps:

1. Start by piercing the carpet near a wall with an awl and pull the goods up off its tack strips until you have access to the back side of the damaged area. Jot down the exact dimensions of your outline.

2. After using your framing square and a utility knife to cut out the damaged area, outline a patch in the same dimensions on the back side of your patch. Note the direction in which the patch's pile will need to run when laying out the outline, then cut the patch with your square and knife.

3. Lay the carpeting back down over the tack strips and carefully insert your patch (check pile direction). Make

sure none of the carpet fibers get folded over.

Now carefully fold back the carpeting, lay seam tape (adhesive side down) along the perimeter of the patch, and heat the tape with an iron until the adhesive melts. (Don't forget to clean your iron while it's still warm.)

4. Weight the taped seams with a heavy object to help

ensure a good bond. Don't disturb the patch for at least 15 minutes.

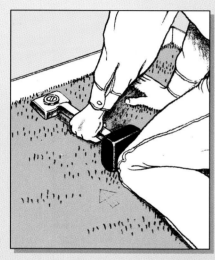

5. To restretch the carpet and fasten it to the tack strips, you'll need a special carpet-laying tool called a knee kicker, which you can rent.

Position the head of the kicker about ¾ inch from the wall and kick its butt end with your knee. Work from each end toward the corner of the room.

TREATING COMMON CARPET STAINS

Stain or Problem	Treatment
463 Wax, tar, grease, chewing gum	Remove as much of the solid as you can by gently scraping with a dull knife or spoon. Treat the stain with dry-cleaning fluid. For chewing gum, apply ice cubes in a plastic bag to harden the gum before scraping.
464 Cigarette burns	Snip off the darkened ends of carpet fibers and gently blot the area with a detergent-vinegar solution (1 teaspoon of each in a quart of warm water). This procedure masks burn damage. For complete repair, patching is necessary.
465 Lipstick	Gently blot the stain with dry-cleaning fluid then with a detergent-vinegar solution. Rinse with a solution of 1 tablespoon of ammonia in a cup of water.
466 Animal stains, fruit juices	If the stain is still wet or fresh, repeatedly sponge it with lukewarm water. Blot dry and treat with a detergent-vinegar solution. Wait 15 minutes, blot again, and sponge the area with clean water. Stains that have changed the carpet's color often cannot be removed.
467 Paint	Treat oil-based paints with turpentine; treat water-based paints with warm water.
468 Ink	Treat ballpoint pen ink by blotting just the ink stain with denatured alcohol. Permanent ink is just what its name implies. Minimize stain by blotting at once with water.
469 For still-wet, unidentified stains	Blot the soiled area with a clean, dry cloth. If there are any solids, remove them with a spoon. Treat the stain with dry-cleaning fluid followed by a solution of detergent and vinegar. Blot again then let the area dry. If needed, reapply whichever cleaner seems to work better. Dry again and brush gently to restore the pile.

This ornate stamped-metal ceiling is original to the Victorian house but it can be easily replicated with new panels of similar design.

470 PRESSED-METAL OPTION

Many people call them tin but pressed-metal ceiling panels are actually lightweight sheets of steel stamped with modular designs. Introduced in the 19th century to cover deteriorated plaster, pressed-metal ceilings have made a comeback and are available in designs that range from Victorian to Art Deco. Keep in mind that a large or ornate design looks best on a high ceiling in a big room. Select smaller, tighter patterns for use on low ceilings. All can be left natural, coated with polyurethane, or painted. If you've never worked with sheet metal before, ask for help. Sharp edges can make the job tricky for a first-timer.

471 CEILING STAIN SOLUTION

You can remove those leak stains on your white ceiling by attacking them with household bleach. Put a small amount of bleach on a cotton ball and dab it on the stain until it's gone. If this doesn't do the trick, cover the spot with stain-killing primer, and then paint.

CAR SIDING IDEAL FOR ATTICS

Car siding—the tongue-and-groove paneled lumber used to construct railroad cars—is great lumber for a farmhouse-style ceiling, especially in attics or on sloped ceilings.

472 Check local lumberyards or home centers for tongue-and-groove boards or panels in a variety of woods—redwood, pine, spruce.

473 Although it's rustic, pine car siding is less expensive than beaded paneling or other wood paneling.

474 Before you begin, insulate between the roof joists and staple up plastic sheeting for a

475 CEILING SAFETY

Many houses today feature ceilings with lumpy textures. Many homeowners dislike this ceiling treatment and want to eliminate it. However, because some acoustical ceiling finishes manufactured before 1978 contain asbestos, take some precautions before scraping. You can send a sample to an EPA-approved testing laboratory. (Check the Yellow Pages and call to learn how to safely obtain a sample.) Or, if you know the builder who built your house, call to learn what ceiling finish was used.

To scrape the ceiling, wear a mask and gloves. Dampen the surface using a spray bottle filled with water. (Add a small amount of soap to the water so the liquid penetrates deeper by breaking surface tension.) Use a putty knife to scrape strips of finish away with one hand and use the other hand to hold a trash basket to catch debris.

vapor barrier. Nail the siding or paneling to the roof joists. Then stain, seal with polyurethane, or paint the ceiling crisp white. To keep white paint from yellowing with age, paint the ceiling boards with an oil-based sealer.

DESIGN IDEA

BONUS STORAGE TRICK

Most houses with a basement have an enormous amount of potential storage space beneath the basement stairs. The trick to using the space efficiently lies in creatively organizing it.

Look closely at the storage closets *below.* They use virtually every cubic inch of storage space under the stairs and are perfect for storing sports equipment. This design calls for box-type storage units to be individually fitted into the slanted space beneath the stairs. These units are set on heavy-duty casters so they slide in and out effortlessly.

Each of these units is made separately. Doors to the units are made of ½-inch plywood. Shelving is made of ¾-inch plywood. Backing for each of the units is perforated hardboard. Rubbing strips on the face of each unit prevent damage when the units are fitted tightly together.

These storage closets use virtually every cubic inch of storage space under the stairs.

476 SIMPLE STEP PAINTING

Painting a set of stairs can be time consuming if you take the typical approach of painting a couple of steps, letting them dry, then painting a couple more. Instead, try painting every other step. Once those are dry, you can paint all of the remaining steps.

SAFETY CONSIDERATIONS

If small children or elderly folks live in your home, you have special reasons to make sure your stair design includes:

477 Handrails designed to be easily grasped. A round profile with a diameter of 1½ to 2 inches provides a good grip.

478 Handrails that extend over every step in the stair run.

479 Balusters that are spaced no more than 4 inches apart.

480 Materials that contrast in both color and texture to signal the beginnings and ends of stairs (such as oak flooring and carpeted stairs).

REPAIRING A HINGED DOOR

Why put up with a loose, squeaky door when the repair could take only a few minutes?

481 Tightening a Hinge

Doors that sag or bind because of hinge-leaf screws that have worked loose in their holes and lost their grip are relatively easy to fix and you needn't remove the door to do it. You should, however, support the door by opening it fully and taping a wedge of wood under the latch edge with a hammer.

Remove the loose hinge-leaf screws and determine whether the leaf will accept larger-diameter screws. If so, install them and retighten the hinge.

If it won't, you can reuse the original screws if you drill out the enlarged screw holes with a ¼-inch bit and hammer in lengths of glue-coated ¼-inch dowel. Then reposition the hinge leaf and secure it by driving the screws into the dowels.

482 Stopping a Squeak

If your hinges are tight but noisy, pry up the hinge pin ¼ inch or so and squirt a few drops

of light oil down into the barrel portion of the hinge, catching excess oil with a rag. Swing the door back and forth.

If the hinge still squeaks, open the door fully, drive a wood wedge under the hinge side, and remove the pin. Clean any rust from the pin with steel wool and from the barrel portion using a stiff, pipe cleaner-type wire brush. Apply a light coat of oil to the pin and replace it. (Don't drive the head of the pin all the way onto the hinge; leave a little space under it for easier removal next time.)

Freeing a Binding Door

If your door binds, first pinpoint the location of the trouble spot while opening and closing the door.

483
If your door is binding on the latch edge, make sure that the hinge leaves on the door or jamb aren't loose. No problem there? Then try shimming out one of the hinges. Shim the top hinge to cure a bind near the bottom and shim the bottom hinge for binds near the top. Here's how.

Open the door and insert a wedge beneath the latch edge of the door. Then remove the screws that hold the doorjamb. Trim a piece of thin cardboard to fit the rectangular mortise on the doorjamb and insert it between the jamb and the hinge leaf.

484
If the top of the door is binding, scribe a line along the door to denote where you want to remove wood. Partially open the door, drive a wedge under its latch edge, and use a block plane to remove the high spot. Work toward the center to avoid splintering the end grain.

485
If the high spot is on the door's bottom edge or along the hinge edge, scribe a line along

487 ENERGY EFFICIENCY

French doors are more energy efficient than sliding glass doors because they exert pressure against the seal when they close. Sliding doors glide against the weather seal and therefore don't provide as tight a seal.

the door's face where you want to remove wood. Tap up on the head of the hinge pins with a hammer and take the door off its hinges for planing.

Anchor the door by wedging one end in a corner or by straddling it. For side planing, work a jack plane in the direction of the grain, holding it at a slight angle to the door. If you're planing end grain at the door's bottom edge, use a block plane and shave toward the center.

486 PICK A POCKET

Inside the house, pick a pocket door and you can add some extra living space. Because pocket doors slide back into the wall—you can gain an extra 4 or 5 square feet of usable floor space everywhere you use one.

488 REPAIRING A LATCH AND STRIKE PLATE

Doors that don't open and close properly are a source of daily irritation and, in some cases, can compromise the security and energy efficiency of your home.

Here are two common problems with a door's strike-latch mechanism and how to correct them.

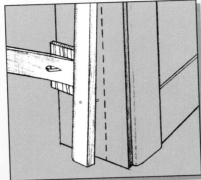

A latch and strike plate that don't quite match up will prevent any door from closing the way it should. To solve the problem, first check to see which edge of the strike the latch is hitting. If only a minor adjustment is necessary, you can remove the strike, as shown *above*. Then put it in a vise and file down the offending edge. Or lengthen the strike mortise and move the strike up or down as needed for a correct fit.

Sometimes, however, a door doesn't close far enough for the latch to engage the strike.

Here, your only alternative is to move the door's stop molding. (This technique also works well for doors that rattle while closed.) Start by carefully prying off the stop molding from the jambs, as shown *above*. Place a scrap of wood between the pry bar and the jamb to prevent damage.

Once you have removed the stop molding, close the door and make a line on the jamb to indicate where the edge of

the stop will be. Then reposition the molding along the line you've drawn, as shown *above*. Finish by painting or staining the area left exposed when you moved the molding.

RESTORING OLD DOORS

Typical door problems include too much paint, frames that have settled, and played-out hardware.

489 Stripping paint is slow, hard work, but you can take doors off their hinges and work outside. Rebuilding door frames that have settled out of square involves removing the molding from at least the top and one side of the door. You then have access to the jamb and can plumb it with wood shims.

490 Some frame pieces may be worn and cracked enough to warrant replacement. In the process, you'll have to realign the strike plate. To do so, reposition it, drill pilot holes, and screw it into place. Then carefully cut around the strike with a utility knife. Remove the plate and chisel away the area within your cuts to the depth of the strike plate. Then reattach the plate.

491 The stiff and paint-encrusted lock will need attention, too. Strip the layers of paint and disassemble and lubricate the mechanism. Broken parts can be replaced with parts scavenged from doors elsewhere in the house. Check out flea markets and garage sales for inexpensive ceramic or glass knobs.

REMODELER'S NOTEBOOK
SKYLIGHT OPTIONS

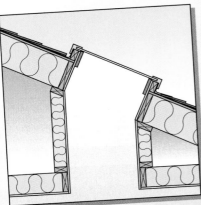

492 **1.** Build a light shaft with sides extending directly downward where you want a spotlight effect, such as over a work area.

494 **3.** For maximum illumination, flare the sides of the shaft so incoming light will reflect off its sides and into the room.

493 **2.** Angle the sides of the shaft if you want to direct the sun's energy to an area that is not directly below the skylight.

496 To keep sliding sashes moving smoothly, clear any paint or debris from the tracks and lubricate with paste wax, paraffin, or silicone lube. To repair the track, unlock and partially open the window then just lift it and flip its lower edge toward you. If the track is bent, cut a wooden block that just fits in the channel then carefully tap the soft metal against it. If all seems clear and straight, lift out of the sash and check its grooved edges. Clean and wax these, too.

497 Bigger windows and sliding glass doors roll on sets of nylon wheels called sheaves. These are self-lubricating and rarely need attention. But if a sheave has been mangled, remove the assembly and replace it.

495 **BRIGHT IDEA**

Shed a little light down under with this idea. A leaf-choked window well is replaced by the sun-scooping greenhouse-style window, *above right.*

The curved glass top welcomes sunshine but turns away tree debris and water. Inside, the deeper, wider window well now sports drywall on the sides and track lighting to shoo away shadows.

ANATOMY OF A WINDOW

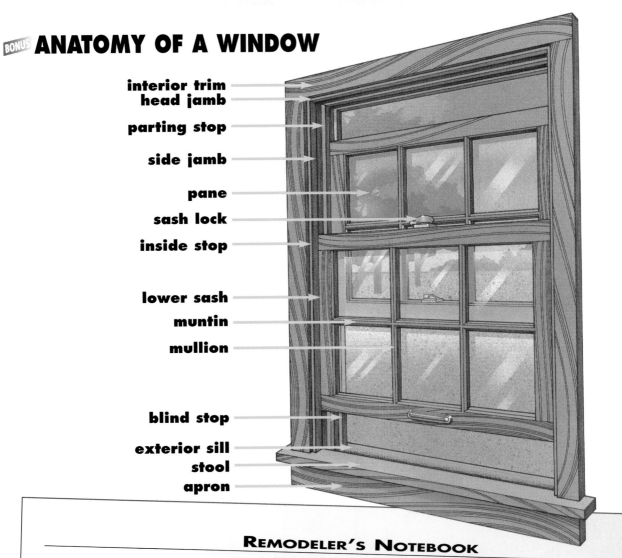

interior trim
head jamb
parting stop
side jamb
pane
sash lock
inside stop
lower sash
muntin
mullion
blind stop
exterior sill
stool
apron

REMODELER'S NOTEBOOK

RESTORING WINDOWS

Nothing establishes the personality of a house like windows. But often the glazing putty is long gone, leaving panes of glass to rattle in the wind. Sashes are painted shut, and sills are cracked and weathered, even on the inside. Counterweight cords may be stiff as pencils or missing altogether.

498 For the price of a putty knife, some glazing points, linseed oil, and glazing putty, you can reglaze your own panes. Restore weathered sashes and sills by brushing boiled linseed oil into the wood. Linseed oil applied beneath the new putty will help it adhere to the wood and window glass.

499 Double-hung windows may have had their counterweight ropes cut and their sashes painted shut. No easy solutions

here, but it is satisfying to get these old things moving again. To get to the counterweights, look for access hatches on the lower sides of the window frames. Pull the weights out. Note the manner by which sash ropes were attached to the window—usually knotted, inserted into a cavity, and nailed in place. Discard any remnants of the old rope through the pulley that's mounted in the frame and down to the counterweight hatch. Raise the window and tie on the counterweight. Wait to trim the excess rope until you are satisfied the weight has enough slack to raise and lower the window.

TRIM TIPS

Professional trim carpenters have a bag full of tricks that simplify their jobs. Here are a few you might try.

500 Spots of glue can mar a finish; a smudge of glue on wood can interfere with stain. So if glue seeps out of a joint, don't wipe it away. Instead, let the glue dry and cut or chip it cleanly away with a chisel.

501 Line your miter box with 100-grit sandpaper to keep molding from slipping while cutting it on an angle.

502 To keep from dimpling the molding with a hammer, leave nails protruding. Sink them with a nail set.

503 Fill gaps in trim joints with surfacing compound and run a bead of latex caulk along ceiling and wall edges. This works only if you plan to paint the trim. It won't work with a stain finish.

504 Paint or stain molding before installing it. Touch up nail holes once the molding is in place.

505 To keep boards from splitting when you nail near the edge, flatten the tip of the nail with a hammer. Or, run the nail through your hair to pick up a little oil.

506 With some materials, particularly hardwoods, pilot holes for nails keep wood from splitting. Make these holes slightly smaller than the nail diameter.

507 Removing molding intact requires patience and care. Because nails holding the molding have been sunk and cavities filled, it's best to drive those nails all the way through with the thinnest possible nail set. Then slip a prying bar beneath the molding near each nail and rock the molding free. If the bar is making indentations

DESIGN IDEA

BONUS ELEVATING THE CEILING

Raising the ceiling and adding a double band of trim elevates views in this kitchen. While the lower molding helps stop the eye, creating a low visual height, the top molding defines the actual room height, thus adding space and intimacy at the same time.

on the wall surface, slip a piece of ¼-inch-thick molding behind it as a buffer.

508 Whenever possible, try to nail your trim at points where there are studs in the wall. This will give a much firmer grip than nailing into drywall only.

509 ## ILLUSION OF HEIGHT

If you want nine- or ten-foot ceilings, consider using crown moldings and headers over doors to give the illusion of height, *right*.

510 SANDING TRICK

PROBLEM: It's difficult to sand the surface of millwork such as quarter-round or cove moldings with conventional flat-faced sanding blocks.

SOLUTION: Custom-make sanding blocks for specific jobs, *above,* using scraps of polystyrene foam. Polystyrene foam is used for packing material or insulation. Look for some small scraps to cut up. Carve or press the foam to the desired shape and fasten sandpaper with double-sided carpet tape. The blocks then fit anything you wish to sand and they're easy to make as you go along.

COPING WITH MOLDING

511 Moldings are the crowning touch to a room and easy to install—until you come to the corners. Here's how carpenters fit those wily curves together.

1. Put the first piece of molding on the wall and nail.

molding. Angle your coping saw back into the bevel as far as you can. The mitered edge is waste to be cut out, leaving a sharp edge on the face of the molding.

2. Position the second piece on a miter box just as it will fit in the wall, only upside down and backward. Cut at a 45-degree angle so that the bottom of the molding (when installed) is longer than the top.

3. With a coping saw, make a cut that traces the outline of the bevel along the face of the

4. Check the fit of the coped edge against the first piece of molding. If any gaps show, fine-tune the coped cut with a file or rasp before nailing in place.

512 **NOTE:** In corners, coped cuts can be used on any curved baseboard, crown, or shoe molding. Coped cuts also make good, clean joints when you're putting moldings end to end.

513 BUILD A BOOKCASE

The patchwork pattern of shelves *below* reflects the informal flavor of the room and is a perfect showcase for books and art objects. Stained wood against a white background frames the owner's collection of folk art. Because the shelves are adjustable, the displays can be changed as often as new items are acquired.

A simple way to install permanent shelves is to butt-join them to vertical members with nails and screws. This method works best for light or moderate loads. For heavier loads such as books, use supports (cleats) made of wood or particleboard about the same thickness as the shelves. Metal clips are also available and provide solid support (they require predrilled holes). Or you can use metal strips and clips for adjustable shelves. It's best to dado the sides of the bookshelves and recess the strips. You can also paint the metal strips to match the wood.

When building a bookcase, use ¾-inch birch plywood; it works well because the grain won't show through a painted finish. If you prefer a stained finish, choose plywood covered with the wood of your choice. For other parts of the bookcase, use dimensional lumber to match the species of plywood you choose.

Size the bookcase and base storage units (if any) to fit your space and to meet your storage needs.

To build storage for electronic gear, measure your television, video, VCR, and stereo components. Then check the owner's manual for each piece of equipment to determine how much ventilation space is needed; some electronic equipment requires several inches. Add the measurements of your equipment to the required ventilation space to determine the minimum size of your base units.

Secure all pieces using wood glue and 6d or 8d finish nails driven slightly below the surface with a nail set. As you work, check your work with a framing square and adjust when necessary. Also, clamp each as needed until the glue is dry before proceeding.

RECOGNIZING QUALITY

When buying cabinetry, visit showrooms and home centers where you can see product displays. To find quality cabinets, look for these features.

514 Top-of-the-line wood cabinets have doors made of solid wood or plywood. Hidden sides, backs, shelves, and drawer parts can be particleboard. For less expense, you'll find doors and frames of plywood, veneered particleboard, or wood-grain laminate.

515 Inspect the wood grain. On quality cabinets, the grain on the doors will match the grain on the frame.

516 With any material, door and drawer edges should be smooth to the touch.

517 If you pull a drawer out about an inch and let go, it should close itself. Self-closing drawers—mounted on a pair of balanced metal slides with ball-bearing rollers—are stronger and smoother than nylon slides or roller mechanisms. When the drawer is fully extended, there should be no side-to-side wavering.

518 Next, look for drawers assembled with screws and dowels rather than glue and staples. Another quality fastening method is called "dovetailing" which is the interlocking of joints.

519 Quality drawer bottoms are as thick as the sides. Bottom panels in drawers should be glued into grooves in the drawer sides, not just stapled.

520 Check knobs and door pulls to be sure the shank of the pull is long enough to accommodate your grasp.

521 Be certain that hidden hinges are adjustable to keep doors aligned. The hinges should also extend beyond 100 degrees to give unhindered access to the inside of the cabinet.

522 NUMBERS TO KNOW

Shelf spans depend on the material you use and the weight of the objects you display. To shelve books, span up to 36 inches using ¾-inch plywood, up to 24 inches using 1-inch lumber, or up to 18 inches using ½-inch glass.

523 HANGING BRACKETS

Wood display shelves look great, especially on wood-paneled walls. But how do you anchor them to the walls without a lot of metal hardware showing?

Rout a stopped groove in the back of your shelf brackets and use that space to make a hidden cleat. Rout the groove, as shown in the illustration *below*. Now cut a cleat that fits snugly into the groove and flush with the back edge of the bracket.

To complete the cleat, cut it in half at a 45 degree angle, screw the bottom, part B, to the wall and glue the top, part A, to the bracket as shown. Slip the bracket over the wall-mounted section of the cleat and you have a strong and completely invisible support.

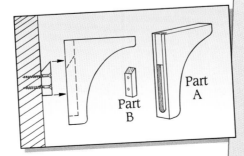

Part B

Part A

524 INSTALLING SHELVES IN A BOOKCASE

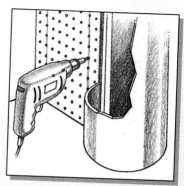

There are many ways to install shelves in a bookcase. If you plan on using purchased pin clips to hold the shelves in place, use a piece of perforated hardboard (with ¼-inch-diameter holes) to ensure accurate spacing without a lot of measuring.

To begin, determine the placement of the pin clips. Measure the distance you want the pin clips from the edges of the bookcase; position the holes about 1 inch in from the front and back edges of the bookcase sides. Trim the perforated hardboard to the width of the bookcase with a hole lining up with the pin-clip location. Position the hardboard, as shown *above*. (To avoid mix ups, mark the top of the guide.)

Wrap electrical tape around the drill bit; this allows you to drill the holes to a uniform depth because the tape stops the penetration of the bit.

FINISHING WOOD

525 SAFE STEPS TO FINISH REMOVAL

Stripping paint and varnish from old furniture isn't difficult. Grab some hopeless garage-sale find, invest a weekend and money for some finish stripper, and turn a cast-off into a keeper.

Chemicals strong enough to dissolve layers of old paint and varnish are toxic and most are flammable as well, so be careful and protect yourself. Methylene chloride fumes pose the biggest health hazard.

• Read instructions carefully before you begin.

• Wear old clothes including a shirt with long sleeves, rubber gloves, and safety goggles.

• Work in a well-ventilated place, taking fresh-air breaks every 10 minutes. Avoid direct sunlight and areas near an open flame. Protect the floor by first spreading a plastic drop cloth, then laying several sheets of newspaper on top.

• Remove all handles, knobs, and latches.

• Pour a small quantity of stripper into a metal—not plastic or glass—container. Use old brushes and throw them away at the end of the day.

• Brush on a generous amount of stripper in one direction only. Don't go back over an area unless the stripper appears to be drying immediately.

• After the surface wrinkles, test a small section with a putty knife, *above right.* If the finish comes right off, remove it from flat surfaces with a putty knife (round the knife's corners to avoid gouging). If some areas hold fast, wait 15 minutes and try again. Manufacturers often

offer several, if not all, of the varieties of finish stripper, so if you're not having much luck with, say, a semipaste, step up to a heavy-paste remover from the same manufacturer. Don't mix brands because some formulas neutralize others.

• After you have removed all the paint or varnish sludge, scrub the stripped piece with fine steel wool soaked in the solvent recommended on the label of the finish stripper.

• When finished, seal the manufacturer's can (virtually all have childproof caps) and store it in a cool, safe place. Periodically check the container for deterioration.

• Dispose of used newspaper and stripping residue as soon as you are finished. Put them in a plastic bag, seal well, and keep away from heat (poke a few holes in the bag for ventilation to prevent spontaneous combustion). Follow local guidelines for disposing of this waste.

SUPERIOR SANDING

When refinishing woodwork, the results will be more satisfactory if the surface is properly prepared.

The simple truth is that sanding is the key to good wood preparation, but deciding what kind of paper and which techniques to use isn't a simple matter at all. That's because the amount of sanding and the type of paper depend on what the surface material is and what is going to be applied to it.

Finishing Wood Doors and Trim

To prevent chipping a new coat of paint or varnish, remove most of the old finish from wood doors, baseboards, windowsills, and window trim.

526 Sanding, rather than scraping, is the better removal method because scraping can damage the wood. You can use a power sander on the doors, but hand-sand the more intricate woodwork and trim to preserve the surface detail. Pull the paper, grit side up, over a sharp edge once or twice to make it pliable when creased for use in grooves.

527 For power sanding a heavy buildup of paint, you'll get good results using disks and belts containing zirconia alumina, an industrial-grade abrasive. Once you're down to the bare wood, use all-purpose sanding discs in medium-grit size to remove any scratches or swirl marks.

Finishing Wood Cabinets

528 Because cabinetry is often made from the softer woods such as pine, garnet abrasive is the best sanding material. It resists loading (filling with sanding residue) and gives a fine, smooth surface to the wood.

529 Begin work with coarse-grit garnet abrasive sheets and decrease the grit size as you work.

OIL FINISH FOR WOOD

Penetrating clear finishes—tung oil, linseed oil, Danish oil, mineral oil, and salad-bowl finish—soak into the pores of wood, forming a finish that resides in the wood itself. You wipe them on with a cloth or the palm of your hand which makes the application practically mistakeproof.

Different products are for different uses. The following information will help you select the right oil for your project.

530 Tung oil comes in two forms—tung oil and polymerized tung oil. Of the two, polymerized dries much faster and has more luster. Both have a light golden color that imparts just the right amount of tone to accent the grain and texture of wooden surfaces. Both form a moisture-resistant, durable coating that dries to a hard, solid film.

531 Linseed oil yields a hand-rubbed look but it has some shortcomings: In addition to its tendency to deepen the color of most woods, it never thoroughly cures and therefore lacks durability. Some furniture builders still stand by boiled linseed oil but most other penetrating oils are superior.

532 Danish oil is a blend of natural oils such as tung and linseed and small amounts of resins. Danish oils create a natural-looking finish superior to pure natural oils alone. They enhance the grain pattern and the texture of the wood while providing a durable finish that's easy to apply and maintain.

533 Oil-varnish mixtures are wipe-on finishes that provide a natural look with more surface protection than pure oils give. The finish is durable, moisture-resistant and easy to apply.

534 Nontoxic finishes are used on wood items that come in contact with food or the mouth such as toys, cutting boards, salad bowls, and wooden utensils. One nontoxic finish, called "salad-bowl" finish, wipes on and can be renewed when necessary. Mineral oil, a common household product, also works as a nontoxic finish. It provides wood with some protection against moisture and wear but it never really hardens.

535 PROS AND CONS OF HEAT STRIPPING

Advantages:
- No chemicals or fumes
- Minimal mess

Disadvantages:
- Slow. You only can strip a small area at a time.
- Careless technique will scorch the wood.
- The heat gun will not remove all the paint and a final application of chemical stripper is usually needed.

Cost:
Approximately $40 to $70 plus electricity. Heat guns are rated at about 1,200 watts; therefore, they use 1.2 kilowatts per hour.

536 CREATE YOUR OWN DIP TANK

Construct a wood box large enough to hold the pieces you want to strip. Line it with heavy plastic—an old water bed liner is perfect. Nail this to the box so that none of the chemical stripper will come in contact with the nails.

PICKING THE RIGHT POLYURETHANE

537 A polyurethane finish provides durability, high or low gloss, and brush-on application making it ideal for the average home woodworker. Some people dislike the "plastic" look of a polyurethane finish but this thick film also provides superior protection against abrasion and water, alcohol, or food stains. Kitchen and bathroom woodwork and cabinets, dining tables, coffee tables, or any surface that sees a lot of spills and hard use deserves a polyurethane finish.

538 Oil-based, wipe-on, and water-based polyurethanes differ significantly in application and performance. Even different brands in the same category may exhibit distinctly different traits so you must match the product to the performance and application characteristics that you need.

539 You may even want to use two different polyurethanes on one project. A table, for instance, may need a durable, alcohol-and-water-resistant polyurethane for the top but a fast-drying product (to prevent runs or sags) for the legs.

PROJECT PRIMER

540 STAINING AND FINISHING WOOD

Gather the following materials:
- [ ] Fine steel wool (0000)
- [ ] Gelled wiping stain or liquid stain
- [ ] Mineral spirits
- [ ] Cotton cloths
- [ ] Varnish or polyurethane finish (for hand-rubbing)
- [ ] Rubber gloves
- [ ] Tack cloth
- [ ] Presealer (optional)

1. Setting up shop: Pick a relatively dust-free workstation with bright light and adequate ventilation. You should be able to leave your project undisturbed for several days to allow for thorough drying or curing.

Clean the surface with mineral spirits on a cotton cloth. Then buff the wood thoroughly with fine steel wool. Soft woods absorb stain unevenly unless they're sealed. To find out if you have a soft wood, push your thumbnail into the surface. If the wood dents, preseal it.

2. Wiping on the stain: Practice staining on scraps of wood and hidden areas of your unfinished piece to be sure you'll get the desired shade.

Apply the stain darker than you want it, using fine steel wool. The stain may appear lighter when dry but the finish coat will restore the color of the wet stain. Allow the stain to penetrate for a few minutes. Use a cotton cloth to wipe away excess stain until you get the desired shade. Stain too dark? Wipe off more. If it's too light, apply another stain coat after the first coat dries thoroughly.

Note: If you don't like the color after you've applied it, you can remove most of the stain with mineral spirits.

Let the stain dry overnight. Then cure the stain under bright, warm light for several hours to ensure dryness. (You may cause smearing if you apply the finish coat or additional coats of stain before the surface is thoroughly dry.) A sunny window or a hanging spotlight are good light sources for this curing step.

3. Hand-rubbing the finish: For the best finishing option, try hand-rubbing. A hand-rubbed finish avoids brush marks and forces the finish well onto the surface.

Wearing rubber gloves and using a cotton cloth, apply the finish with the palm of your hand. Allow the finish to dry thoroughly. Buff with fine steel wool to smooth uneven spots. Brush away dust with a tack cloth or vacuum the surface. Apply a second finish coat. If you're finishing an open-grain wood such as oak, or applying varnish to a surface that will get heavy use, apply three or more coats.

541 GEL STAINS

Gel stains top the list of foolproof stains. These puddinglike products rub on with a soft cloth and dry in 2 to 24 hours in smooth, even coats. One favorite is Wood-Kote's Fruitwood, which gives a warm, rich glow. Other beauties: Pennsylvania Cherry from Bartley and Mediterranean Oak from Formby's. These products require finish coats of polyurethane or tung oil to protect the wood.

Gel stains are neat, too. They require only a few seconds of shaking to mix. This lets you skip the drippy task of stirring that comes with liquid stains. The squeezable plastic bottles are easy to handle.

Complete project kits simplify shopping for a first-timer. Bartley's kit includes gel stain, a gel varnish, sandpaper, gloves, and four soft cloths.

542 BLEACH OUT BLACK MARKS

To remove black water marks from bare wood that will be refinished, mix 1 tablespoon of oxalic acid powder with ½ to 1 cup of water. Apply with a soft cloth and rub. Repeat if necessary. Let the wood dry thoroughly before sealing.

543 NUMBERS TO KNOW

To outfit closets, hang a single rod at a height of 63 to 72 inches. For double rods, install the top rod 76 to 84 inches high and the lower rod at 36 to 42 inches high.

CONTROL CLUTTER

Even the best organizing system can't save a closet that's packed with last year's tax records and a wardrobe from 10 pounds ago.

Start organizing your closet by giving away clothes you don't wear and by storing out-of-season garments in boxes under the bed. Then turn to hardware stores or closet boutiques for help. You can buy do-it-yourself systems prepackaged for standard closets, design your own closet system with off-the-shelf components, or hire a custom-closet firm to do it for you.

The illustration at *right* offers ideas on organizing a reach-in closet. Outfitted with a wire storage system, it shows the four basics of closet organization.

544 A double-rod hanging compartment for blouses, skirts, and slacks. By stacking one closet rod above another, double hanging takes advantage of wasted vertical space and multiplies hanging capacity. In this closet, shirts and tops are grouped on the high rod, with skirts below. Outfits can be coordinated at a glance.

545 A single-rod hanging compartment for dresses and robes. A must for women's closets, this area can be compressed or eliminated for men. Ventilated systems let you adjust the amount of this storage through time.

546 Eye-level storage for folded items. The strategy is to keep your belongings where you will see and use them. If you see it, you wear it. Closet drawers are only needed for socks and underwear. In this reach-in closet, a tier of shelves and see-through drawers keeps clothes in plain view.

547 Accessory storage. Prevent a jumble of shoes on the floor with a shoe storage system. Add a few wire organizers for ties, belts, and other clutter culprits.

Measurements

The following guidelines will get you started but you'll want to adjust them to your own wardrobe and storage preferences. Also consider your height and the reaches that are comfortable for you.

548 Hang clothes rods at least 12 inches from the back of the closet to allow for the width of the hanger and garment.

549 For shelf-and-rod installations, leave a minimum 3-inch clearance between the rod and the shelf so you can move hangers easily.

550 Makers of ventilated storage systems recommend you space shelves at least 13 inches apart. Otherwise space shelves according to what will be stored on them; include 2 to 3 inches of room above the top item.

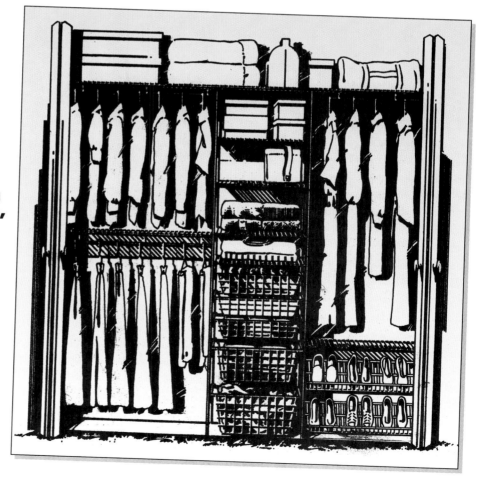

SIZE UP THE ATTIC

Appraise your attic's finishing potential using this set of guidelines.

551 You may need to improve or relocate the entrance to your attic. Plan at least a 3x10-foot rectangle for a standard stairway or a 5½-foot square for a spiral unit. To make room for stairs, look for a closet you can cut down, tuck a spiral staircase into a corner, or add a corner. Where you place stairs depends on available headroom.

552 Ask an architect or building contractor to check the floors for strength and movement. If they give much, double up each joist, especially where joists run for long distances or support heavy objects.

553 If you have a forced-air heating system, heat the attic by extending runs from the level below or install an auxiliary unit. You also may need to reinsulate.

554 Make sure your plans meet all building, electrical, and fire codes. For example, your attic will probably need a certain number of square feet of window space.

BONUS If your attic doesn't measure up, count on making some structural changes to the floor, walls, and ceiling. The illustration *(right)* shows five areas that may require alterations.

A finished attic can be a hot property in your home. A finished, poorly insulated attic can be even hotter—up to 140 degrees in the summer.

555 Proper insulation can keep you comfortable year-round. How much you need depends on your climate. In general, the U.S. Department of Energy recommends:

• R-values (the resistance to heat flow) of about R-11 to R-19 in walls. Usually a 2x4 wall can hold up to R-13 insulation; a 2x6 wall can hold up to R-19 insulation.

• About R-19 to R-38 in attic ceilings. This insulation can be up to 12 inches thick.

Keep these tips in mind:

556 Caulk and plug air leaks before you insulate.

557 Many insulation products come with a vapor-barrier backing. Otherwise a sheet of 2-mil polyethylene or foil-backed gypsum wallboard can protect against moisture.

558 Finished attics need insulation between the studs of knee walls and exterior walls and between ceiling rafters. Spacers help provide a snug fit for the insulation.

559 Separate pieces of insulation can fit more tightly than a continuous roll at joints.

560 Provide enough ventilation by allowing at least 1 inch of air space between the insulation and the roof sheathing.

561 Staple the insulation in place to hold it firmly.

562 Faced insulation should not be left exposed.

563 Insulation should be installed firmly but not packed. Wedging an extra dose of insulation into an already filled space may compress air pockets in the insulation and actually reduce its R-value.

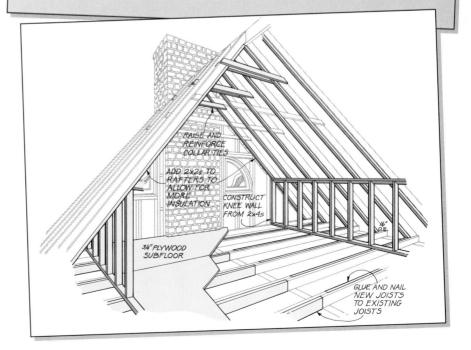

CANDIDATES FOR CONVERSION

564 In order to convert your attic to living space it needs to be supported with conventional framing. How can you tell? Use a flashlight to inspect the configuration of the rafters. If your attic looks similar to the illustration *at right,* then you're in luck. Deep-six remodeling plans if you discover a series of zigzag trusses filling the attic cavity.

565 Most building codes also require the ceiling to be at least 7½ feet high over 50 percent of the floor area.

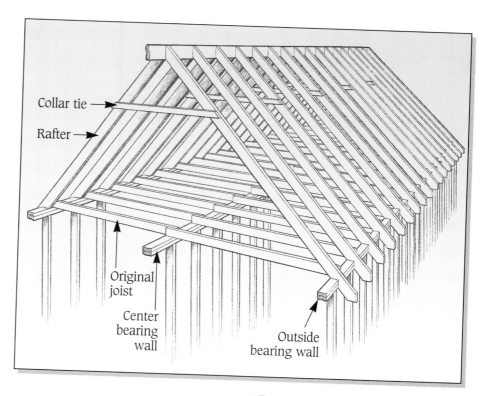

566 In conventional attic framing, the weight of the roof and ceiling rests on bearing walls. Joists overlap at the center wall. Collar beams hold the rafters together.

567 ADDING COLLAR TIES

To make room for a bedroom in the attic, the roof was first taken off this house and collar ties added. Anytime you open up roof framing like this, you must have a collar tie. It keeps the sides of the roof rafters from flattening out. The open ceiling gives the bedroom a spacious feel without making the house too tall to fit into the neighborhood. Exposed collar beams add architectural interest.

BASEMENTS

DEALING WITH MOISTURE

568 Here's a foolproof way to tell if basement moisture is outside seepage or inside condensation. Tape a piece of aluminum foil to the basement wall where you experience the most moisture. Use duct tape and leave a small air space on the inside of the foil. After 48 hours remove the foil. If there is moisture on the inside of the foil, the problem is seepage. If the moisture is on the outside of the foil, the problem is condensation.

569 Condensation usually can be cured by using a dehumidifier. Seepage is the result of outside water leaking into your basement through cracks in the walls. A mild case of seepage may require only some waterproofing on the inside of the basement walls. Serious problems require professional help.

DRY BASEMENT CHECKLIST

Don't let a wet basement dampen your spirits. Ninety-five percent of all basement water problems are entirely curable—mostly by surprisingly simple and inexpensive methods. Here are some steps to try before calling the contractor.

570 Clean out the gutters. Keep your gutters free from leaves, twigs, and other debris so water won't overflow and seep into the basement. Extend downspouts at least 10 feet away from the house to avoid water accumulation near the foundation.

571 Improve your grades. If you find puddles at your foundation during heavy rains, chances are your yard needs to be regraded. In fact, poor grading and improper backfill are the most common causes of basement water. Ground at the foundation should slope away from the house. Ten feet from the foundation, the lawn should be about one foot lower than the ground surrounding the house.

572 Look at your landscaping. Remove trees planted within 10 feet of the house because they may crack the basement walls and clog drainage tile. Also remove flower beds close to the foundation walls; they may collect water and allow it to seep inside.

573 Watch those window wells. Stop water from entering through your basement windows by building window wells that are at least 4 inches above the grade. Inexpensive plastic domes will also prevent water seepage.

574 An inside approach. For the 5 percent of basement water problems caused by a high water table rather than surface water, the answer may be to fit your basement with an interior system that traps incoming water and channels it to a sump pump. Interior dampness problems often can be solved from the inside. Use waterproof concrete to patch cracks and waterproof paint to limit seepage.

SAFETY

FIRE FIGHTERS

For safety's sake, every home needs a fire extinguisher. But if the nitty-gritty of choosing one leaves you cold, take a look at our red-hot guide.

What Kind?

575 Extinguishers carry labels to tell you what kinds of fires they can fight:
A: Paper, wood, cloth, rubber, upholstery, and other dry combustibles.
B: Oil, grease, gasoline, and other flammable liquids.
C: Appliances, TVs, and other electrical equipment.

Combination ABC extinguishers are popular for home use. Sleek, lightweight BC kitchen extinguishers are widely available now. Numbers indicate the relative extinguishing potential. Ask a dealer to help you choose the rating you need. In a large house, you may want two different extinguishers tailored to the needs of specific rooms.

576 Most homeowners choose dry chemical extinguishers because this type is versatile and inexpensive. Halon extinguishers are catching on for home use, too, especially around computers and home offices because they won't damage equipment or records. Colorless, odorless halon gasses extinguish fires and then evaporate, leaving no stains or residue. However, halon extinguishers cost more than their dry chemical cousins and they use ozone-depleting chemicals, making them harmful to the environment.

577 How Many Do I Need and Where?

In a small to average-size house, one fire extinguisher is usually enough. In a large home, buy one for each floor. Mount extinguishers in plain view, away from cooktops and fireplaces. Another smart idea is to choose a spot near a room exit so you can reach the extinguisher safely and bail out if the fire gets out of hand.

578 How Much?

Prices from $10 to $30 are common for dry-chemical home extinguishers. For a halon extinguisher, you can expect to spend from $20 to $50. A well-stocked hardware store or home center will carry most types.

What About Maintenance?

579 Pressure gauges tell you if your extinguisher will work; check your gauge routinely. Most home models are made to be thrown away rather than refilled after use.

580 A final note: Don't rely on your extinguisher to save lives. In the event of a fire, get everyone out of the house and have someone call the fire department. Use your fire extinguisher to save property only if the blaze is confined to its area of origin.

FIRE SAFETY

BONUS HOW TO USE FIRE EXTINGUISHERS

To work most fire extinguishers, think of the word "pass:"

Pull the pin. You may need to release a lock latch or press a puncture lever first.

Aim the nozzle, horn, or hose.

Squeeze or press the handle.

Sweep from side to side at the base of the fire until it goes out. Watch to make sure the fire doesn't reignite.

Check the instructions on your extinguisher for variations.

ADDING ON

581 Add-on alternatives.
Before beginning a major
addition, consider all your
options. Decide whether
finishing the basement or attic,
enclosing a porch, rearranging
interior walls, or annexing your
garage would offer extra living
space more inexpensively.

**582 Invest in good
design.** If you decide to add
on, be sure to invest in a
quality design. A well-
integrated addition can improve
the attractiveness and value of
your home. But one that
appears tacked on can decrease
your home's worth.

**583 Choose your
approach.** If your house has
distinctive architecture, consider
imitating its styling. If you
want to add a more
contemporary addition to an
older home, tie the two together
by echoing the basic massing,
roof line, materials, and
detailing. With a bland or
featureless home, consider
building a stylish addition to
create character and
excitement.

584 It's in the material.
You can match the original
exactly or choose
complementary or contrasting
materials. Whatever route you
take, buy new materials of the
same quality as the originals.
Be sure that trim work,
windows, and doors blend with
the original details.

**585 Consider your
comfort.** An addition can
look as though it has always
been there yet feel added on.
Check into upgrading your
furnace, air-conditioning, and
water heater so that new rooms
are as comfortable as old ones.

Shhh! CONTROL HOUSEHOLD NOISE

Homes built closer together,
smaller in square footage, and
with more "open" living spaces,
make it harder to get away from
the sounds of the family,
neighbors, and automobile and
air traffic. The "sounds of
silence" are in greater demand
as people seek refuge from the
daily grind.

Material Concerns

586 Construction products are
available to control inside and
outside sound. Laminated
glass—similar to that used in car
windshields—reduces outside
noise better than ordinary glass.
It is manufactured through a
multistep process that involves
bonding a plastic sheet, or
interlayer, between two or more
panes of glass. The interlayer
dampens sound.

587 Sound-control mortar applied
during the installation of ceramic
tile or natural stone can help
reduce noise. Also on the market
are sound-deadening boards and
underlayment for use beneath a
variety of flooring materials.
Structural sound-control boards
are specially made for use as a
noise-deadening component in
room partitions and peripheral
walls.

Construction Approaches

588 Certain construction
techniques can solve noise
problems without the expense of
specialty products. Some of
these acoustical approaches
include:

• Making floor joists one size
deeper than required.
• Using double-stud walls or
resilient clips and acoustical
batts.
• Sealing all openings.
• Staggering electrical outlet
boxes in walls between rooms or
in walls separating different
units of a multifamily home.
• Using more standard
insulation.
• Insulating with soft
furnishings—carpeting, area
rugs, and fabric.

589 One of the most common
ways of absorbing sound on the
interior is with soft goods.
Simply using carpeting and area
rugs over hard surfaces and
purchasing fabric rather than
leather upholstery makes a big
difference in sound transmission.

590 Another design idea gaining
popularity is the "padded wall."
This involves stapling a thin

HIRING A PRO: CONTRACTS

Horror stories from people who have hired contractors without detailed contracts would rival the works of Stephen King. Never proceed in any remodeling job without a contract that carefully outlines what you expect in materials, performance, and completion schedule. No matter what size the job, don't rely on good rapport with a contractor to settle disagreements.

Your builder might make replacing a window look easy with plans he draws on a doughnut bag but what happens when simple projects turn complicated? Your house may have rotting studs that have to be replaced. Or perhaps your siding is a type no longer made and has to be patched with costly special-order material.

A simple contract establishes guidelines for responsibility and liability. An attorney is the best source of advice but here are some points to watch for:

592 Contracts should specify what materials will be used, right down to the drywall thickness and plywood rating. Good contracts also include clear drawings of the work to be done and a one-year warranty. Many builders try to get away with a 60-day warranty.

593 Make sure the contract permits you to withhold payment. The builder will want progress payments with the start of a job phase but try to make payments at the completion of a job phase. If you are not satisfied, withhold a partial payment until the problem is fixed.

594 Formalize in your contract when your "punch list" will be presented. A punch list details the little nicks and dents that need to be fixed before the builder receives final payment. The list should include touch-up painting, doors that stick, or last-minute caulking.

595 Don't agree to large payments—over 33 percent of the total payment—up front, with progressively smaller payments. If you have a disagreement at the end of the job, the builder has little to lose by walking away from repairs that will cost more than the final payment.

596 Ask the contractor to designate an official "contact" who can speak with you about your concerns. Families should also designate a single individual to make periodic quality checks and discuss problems with the builder.

597 Don't worry about surprises during the building process—expect them. You might want an extra skylight or the builder may discover hidden termite damage that has to be corrected before the project can proceed.

Use written change orders for extra things you want done. When making change orders, keep a dated, written record and provide a copy to your contractor. The change order should specify the item number of any products involved beyond the original contract, the cost, and any schedule adjustments required to complete the work. Make sure your builder uses change orders to obtain your approval for extra charges such as those commonly cited as "hidden conditions."

598 Insist on a building permit, even if the builder discourages this. A job with a permit gets checked by your local building inspector, giving you a trained eye to make sure everything is up to code. That's especially important with your electrical and plumbing work. Permits are an added expense that varies by municipality and they involve a waiting period but think of them as preventive medicine.

599 Don't be shy about questioning contract clauses; insist that materials be spelled out in the contract and check job performance. Beware of the phrase "equal or better" or you could end up with inferior materials. Agree in advance on the materials and products you want.

---

sheet of polyester batting—the type commonly sold in fabric stores—to the wall and covering the pad with fabric sewn to suit the size of the wall. Edges of the fabric, also stapled in place, are covered with decorative trim strips.

The padding keeps sound out but also helps keep sound in, a plus for areas such as media rooms. The drawback is that the wall must be cleaned professionally, similar to an upholstered piece of furniture.

If there is enough air space around your windows, you can use multilayer window treatments. Usually these consist of an underdrapery, some space between it and the window, and an overdrapery.

10 COMMON CODE VIOLATIONS AND HOW TO AVOID THEM

According to city and county building officials, these are the 10 most common code violations. Some can be easily corrected; others could require extremely expensive alterations.

600 1. Improper spacing of anchor bolts in the foundation wall (should be spaced 12 inches in from each end and a maximum of 6 feet apart).

601 2. Improper lumber for plates used at the junction between wall and foundation (wooden plates should be resistant to rot and insects).

602 3. Excessive notching of floor joists or wall framing to make room for plumbing drains (rules vary; contact your local building department).

603 4. Wiring or plumbing closer than ⅝ inch to the edge of a framing member. (If closer than this distance, the framing edge should be covered with metal to prevent an electrical short or water leak caused by a drywall nail or screw.)

604 5. Lack of a proper-size emergency fire-exit window (should be 6 square feet, at least 20 inches wide, 24 inches high, and no more than 44 inches above the floor).

605 6. Errors with stairways (should have at least 6 feet 8 inches of vertical clearance from the front edge of any step to the ceiling; stairways with three steps or more should have a railing located 30 to 34 inches above the tread).

606 7. Lack of safety glass near doors or around tub and shower enclosures (rules vary; contact your local building department).

607 8. Lack of adequate space between incandescent light bulbs and shelving in closets. (Incandescent bulbs should be at least 12 inches away from edge of shelf; fluorescent bulbs can be 6 inches from shelf.)

608 9. Lack of adequate drainage away from the building. (Make sure gutters are working properly and build up soil around foundation so it slopes away from the house.)

609 10. Lack of stamped, approved plans on site when the inspector arrives. (An easy violation to avoid; just make sure to have the plans on hand.)

MONEY $ MATTERS
HOW TO SAVE ON LABOR AND MATERIALS

Even if you're not an experienced remodeler, there are jobs you can do yourself that will allow you to stretch your budget. You can also save on materials by shopping carefully and keeping your eyes open for bargains and possible discounts.

610 Handle labor-intensive work like tearing out, painting, insulation, and cleanup yourself.

611 Plan your remodeling around existing plumbing features and gas lines. Changing these is expensive.

612 Order lumber from a mill. If you need less than the minimum truckload a mill will sell, combine orders with a friend or another remodeler your contractor knows about.

613 Establish your total budget and stick to it. If you splurge on a major appliance, for example, control spending on cabinets and/or fixtures to balance the budget.

614 Buy seconds (products with slight flaws) direct from the manufacturer.

615 Purchase materials during the off-season, when prices are lower.

616 Take advantage of clearance sales on insulation, wiring, paint, etc.

617 Ask your contractor to pass along to you the discount (usually 10 percent) that dealers give contractors on large purchases of building supplies.

618 Ask the contractor which cabinet styles are easiest and cheapest to install before making your choice.

619 Don't make changes in design plans once the project is started. Change-order labor and materials will cost you extra.

620 You'll avoid paying the middleman's fee charged by professionals if you do your own contracting. But this route isn't for everyone. Serving as your own general contractor means that you have to bid jobs and/or negotiate fees and terms for yourself and be responsible for scheduling, supervising, and paying subcontractors.

KITCHENS AND BATHS
KITCHENS: DESIGN

PLANNING THE PERFECT KITCHEN

BONUS Kitchen-practical black and white vinyl tiles point the way to an adjacent dining area and to the wood strip flooring that continues through the rest of the house. The classic checkerboard pattern looks contemporary when laid diagonally.

Floor Plan—
There are three basic kitchen floor plans.

U-shape is the most efficient because it prevents traffic from cutting through the work triangle. You'll need a kitchen that is at least 8 feet square to provide the minimum of 4 feet central working area.

L-shape is often the easiest layout to work with if you aren't adding square footage. With cabinets and appliances located at right angles on adjacent walls, it's ideal for a family that likes to congregate in the kitchen. The work triangle is compact and enough space remains for a dining table and chairs.

Corridor or galley is common in older houses and apartments. The best arrangement places the refrigerator and sink on one wall and the range on the opposite wall. The aisle between counters should measure not less than 4 feet and not more than 6 feet.

621 Countertops The key to a workable, efficient kitchen is to have as much uninterrupted counter space as possible. It doesn't have to be in a straight run; it can turn a corner, just so it's continuous.

622 Flooring Hardwood makes a good kitchen floor because it has a natural "give." A new product called Marmoleum looks like old-fashioned linoleum, wears like the best grade vinyl, and is all natural—a cork base with jute backing. Marmoleum requires minimum maintenance and will look new for many years.

623 Lighting Try combining kinds of lighting. Ceiling lights, for example, can be recessed cans with halogen bulbs giving a bright, white, energy-efficient light. Because the light is so bright, fewer cans can be used. Low-voltage halogens make good under-cabinet lighting. If you want softer light, use halogen in the ceiling and low-voltage incandescent lights under the cabinets.

624 Recent trends Recent trends in kitchen design include built-in recycling centers, eat-in spaces with a table and chairs, planning centers with a desk, and side-by-side refrigerator/-freezers. If you're planning to resell soon, it's a good idea to incorporate at least one of these into your kitchen to add to its appeal.

KEEPING YOUR KITCHEN CLEAN

625 High-gloss surfaces show dirt faster and require more upkeep. Specify matte finishes for countertops, appliances, and flooring.

626 Avoid resilient flooring with a pebbly finish. Dirt sticks in the crevasses, making the floor harder to clean.

627 A halogen cooktop means no burners to clean.

628 Glass-shelved refrigerators confine spills and are easier to wipe down.

629 Flush-set or undermounted sinks let you wipe crumbs and spills into the sink directly from the countertop.

630 A coved backsplash is easier to clean.

631 Almost all cabinet manufacturers offer a range of organizers to make the kitchen neater. You can incorporate storage dividers, lazy Susans, recycling bins, towel racks, message centers, cookbook holders, spice racks, even metal-lined bread drawers.

632 Your kitchen range hood must be vented to the outdoors (some merely pull the grease and smoke up and blow it back into the room). And be sure the fan is strong enough, especially if you have a downdraft range.

633 Have the dishwasher mounted a foot or two off the floor (you can put cabinets above it) to save you from having to bend over to load and unload.

REMODELER'S NOTEBOOK

BONUS KITCHEN COST UPDATE

Remodeling a kitchen involves major expense and requires careful planning to avoid over-stretching one's budget or compromising on quality. A percentage breakdown of expenses shows where remodeling dollars go.

Cabinets	43%
Labor	21%
Countertops	12%
Appliances	8%
Fixtures/Fittings	5%
Flooring	4%
Lighting	3%
Miscellaneous	4%

BONUS FLOOR PLANS

The work triangle, as indicated by the shaded area in the following floor plans, connects the kitchen's three major work centers—cooktop or range, refrigerator, and sink. Ideally, the sides of the triangle should total between 12 and 22 feet. If the triangle measures less, the kitchen is probably cramped; if the triangle measures more, you'll add needless mileage to kitchen chores. The best floor plans prevent traffic from cutting through the work triangle.

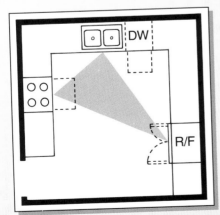

U-Shape

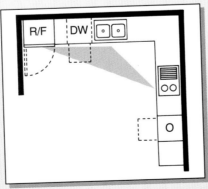

L-Shape

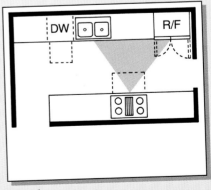

Corridor

MAKE EVERY INCH COUNT

Incorporate some of the following ideas into your kitchen for extra storage space.

634 Keep small appliances out of sight, but convenient in an appliance garage (back wall of photo). Include electrical outlets in the garage and a door to keep things out of sight when not in use.

635 A sliver of space as narrow as 6 inches can be turned into a pullout pantry for storing cans and spices; 9 inches is enough room for a cookie-sheet cabinet.

636 Slots in the back of the counter can provide convenient storage for knives.

637 Create a niche between wall studs by building shelves to use for display or to hold spices.

638 Swing-out shelves and lazy Susans make good use of corner cabinets. Pullout trays help you easily see items stored at the back of cabinets.

CUTTING CABINET COSTS

Don't cut corners on cabinets. Follow these tips to get what you want for less.

640 Select the larger cabinet sizes where possible (one 48-inch-wide unit is less expensive than two 24-inch units, for example).

641 Choose less expensive doors from a quality line.

642 Install glass doors in one area only.

643 Avoid custom-made interior equipment.

644 Add storage aids to the cabinets later.

639 DESIGN IT RIGHT

Design it right—the first time. Planning ahead can save a significant amount of remodeling money. Before you seek design help, put your own ideas on paper. List what it is you like about your present kitchen and what you really want to change. Rank those items you'd like to change in order of priority: You may be able to accomplish some goals now and save some for later. Once you know what you want, take your ideas to a designer and ask for a quote. If what you have in mind costs more than you're able to spend, ask your planner to help you pare down costs based on your list of priorities.

An extra sink in the island, ample counter space, and glass-front bins can boost a kitchen's efficiency.

645 COOK UP A GREAT KITCHEN

Just like a favorite recipe, a kitchen remodeling plan requires the proper ingredients for appealing results. After surveying a lot of homeowners with terrific kitchens, we found ten features they appreciated most. Put them on your list, too.

1. Efficient floor plan and easy traffic flow. Strive for a compact work triangle connecting the refrigerator, range, and sink, and a plan that directs household traffic away from the work core.

2. An island paradise. If you have the space, an island serves as a workstation, a storage area, and a lunch counter.

3. Storage, storage, storage. Assess your possessions and the amount of groceries you keep on hand then plan storage to fit. Special features, such as a pantry and a recycling center, customize your kitchen to suit you.

4. A gathering place. Today, most cooks don't want to be left out of the activity. That's why kitchens that open to the family room rank high on remodelers' wish lists.

5. Let the sunshine in. Nothing adds cheer to a kitchen more effectively than a lot of windows and a skylight or two.

6. Lights, please. Nobody likes working in their own shadow. Plan for lighting that glows on all work surfaces.

7. Character building. Call it beauty, charm, or personality. It's one way homeowners express their individuality and welcome visitors. Cozy seating areas, fireplaces, and fancy finishes all add to it.

8. Let's eat in. With their fast-paced lifestyles, today's families are rediscovering the importance of togetherness—around the kitchen table.

9. Durable materials. Well-planned kitchens feature durable, easy-maintenance materials for floors, countertops, and cabinets.

10. Something special. Be sure to treat yourself to that one amenity you've always wanted. For some, it's a water-and-ice dispenser in the refrigerator door. For others, it's an instant hot water spout at the kitchen sink.

NUMBERS TO KNOW

Add these basic measurements to your plans and see how they help your kitchen measure up.

Mixing-center basics

646 Plan for 36 to 42 inches of uninterrupted counter space.

647 Allow 28 to 30 inches for a refrigerator with a top freezer 30 to 36 inches for a side-by-side refrigerator/freezer.

Cooking-center basics

648 Make sure an overhead cabinet is 27 to 36 inches above a cooktop.

649 The open height of a wall-oven door should be 5 to 7 inches below the cook's elbow.

Cleanup-center basics

650 Purchase a 36-inch base cabinet for a double sink or a 30-inch base cabinet for a single sink.

651 Allow an 18- or 24-inch-wide space for an automatic dishwasher.

652 An overhead cabinet should be at least 22 inches above the sink.

Baking-center basics

653 Plan 36 to 42 inches of uninterrupted counter space between the oven and the refrigerator.

654 Set the counter 3 to 6 inches lower than a standard counter for ease in rolling out dough.

655 Plan a 30-inch-deep counter for extra room.

Planning-center basics

656 Make room for a desk at least 24 inches wide and 20 inches deep.

657 Allow 30 inches of clearance for pulling out the chair.

Eating-counter basics

658 Plan a slice of counter 24 to 30 inches wide and at least 15 inches deep for each person.

659 Stools should leave 12 to 18 inches of knee space between the top of the stool and the bottom of the counter.

660 RECYCLE IT

No excuses for not recycling in this home. The recycling bins stop a little short of the countertop so you can toss in containers without even opening a door. The trio of bins are located at the end of the kitchen island where they're handy to both the eating area and the cooking center. Standard brown paper grocery bags fit into the bins.

COPING WITH COOKING DURING A KITCHEN REMODELING

With a little ingenuity and a lot of flexibility, you can still perform as chief cook and bottle washer.

661 Move the refrigerator into the next room or a nearby hallway, away from workers and the dust they create.

662 Pack and store all but a few essential pans, dishes, and kitchen accessories.

663 Set up a "field kitchen" in an entryway, on the deck (if it's covered), in the dining room, or in the basement. Equip it with a table, a cutting board, dishpans, and a garbage can. Remember, you probably won't have access to the garbage disposal.

664 Plan simple meals. Cook on a grill, in an electric cooking pot, or on a hot plate.

BONUS ISLAND ON WHEELS

Red rubber wheels keep this kitchen island on the move or lock it in place when it's needed for a breakfast bar.

Adapt this idea for use at your house by adding wheels to standard cabinetry and top it off with a countertop.

665 Buy take-out salads and desserts at the supermarket.

666 Use paper plates and cups.

667 Wash dishes in the laundry room or bathroom. Simply carry them in dishpans from your temporary kitchen to the dishwashing area.

KITCHENS: APPLIANCES

668 OVEN THERMOSTAT

When an electric oven doesn't heat correctly, it just takes common sense to tell whether an element or the thermostat failed. Test for a failed element by setting the oven control to "bake" at 350 degrees. Within minutes, the baking element should glow red. Set the control to "broil" to test the broiler element. A failed thermostat results in no heat or inaccurate temperatures.

669 SHARPENING DISPOSAL BLADES

If you've ever wondered how you might sharpen the blades on your garbage disposal, you needn't. The grind wheel blades and the teeth of the shredder ring never need sharpening if the disposal is operated according to the manufacturer's instructions. Owners of heavy-duty disposals occasionally should grind bones in their units to remove any buildup of food soils.

BUILDING IN THE MICROWAVE

670 Consider the height of the people who will use the oven. For example, don't install one in your upper cabinets if you expect children to use it.

671 Be sure your oven's door works with the location. For instance, a high location calls for an oven with a door that opens to the side rather than one that pulls down, and presents an awkward reach to retrieve a hot dish.

672 A microwave oven needs air circulation to cool the tubes. Your owner's manual or dealer will tell you how many inches of air space to allow around the sides, the top, and the bottom of the oven.

673 When installing a microwave oven above or below a thermal or convection oven, see if you need a heat deflector to protect the microwave oven from the heat of the other oven.

SMART APPLIANCE BUYS

To get the most from your appliances for the space they consume, consider these options:

674 Put your emphasis on refrigerator/freezer space. Today people use more fresh, refrigerated, and frozen foods than canned and dried foods but most cabinet recommendations are based on a time when the reverse was true. Adjust to reality and give up cabinet space for refrigerator/freezer space.

675 Purchase a combination microwave/electric, gas/convection, or microwave/convection oven if you don't have space in your kitchen for two separate ovens.

676 Install a 30-inch downdraft range to get a grill-griddle feature in addition to a four-burner cooktop.

677 Select a single-bowl sink with a drain board that fits over a dishwasher if there isn't enough side-by-side space for a double-bowl sink and dishwasher. This makes sense because dishwashers reduce the need for double-bowl sinks.

TROUBLESHOOTING A DISPOSAL

The symptoms of a food waste disposal problem—a loud clanking noise, the strained buzz of an electric motor, or no action at all—get your attention. Fortunately, the symptoms often are worse than the illness.

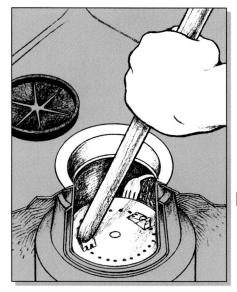

678 **1. Removing an obstruction.** Jams are caused by obstructions within the disposal. You'll recognize the problem right away by the commotion it makes when the unit is turned on. If your unit jams, shut off its power source immediately. Then remove the splash guard and survey the situation. Once you locate the obstruction, insert the end of a broom or mop handle or a large dowel into the grinding chamber. Pry against the turntable until it rotates freely. Remove the obstruction from the chamber.

With one brand of disposal, you insert an allen wrench into a hole in the bottom of the disposal and work the tool back and forth. Then remove the obstruction.

An impossible jam requires professional attention.

679 **2. Restarting the motor.** When the motor shuts off while the disposal is operating, it's probably because the overload protector sensed overheating and broke electrical contact. To reactivate the motor, wait about five minutes for it to cool, then push the reset button located on the bottom of the disposal.

If the unit won't start, make sure the fuse or circuit breaker controlling the flow of power to the disposal is functioning. Be sure the unit is plugged in or otherwise connected to the power source.

680 **3. Clearing a clogged drain.** Because a disposal gobbles up huge amounts of food waste, it's to be expected that occasionally the drain line may clog. If this happens, unplug the disposal, place a pan or bucket beneath the trap to catch the water that will spill, and disassemble the trap.

If the trap itself is clear, thread a drain auger into the drainpipe and work it back and forth until the drain is clear.

681 **CAUTION:** Never attempt to clear a blocked drain line with chemicals of any type. If the solution doesn't work, you'll have a drain line filled with caustic chemicals.

The cleared drain is less likely to clog again if you always use cold water when operating the disposal and if you run both the disposal and the water for a full minute after all the food has been ground.

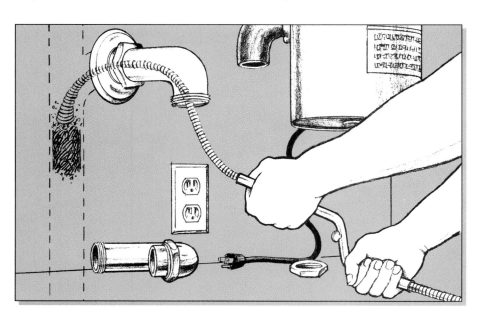

SOLVING DISHWASHER WOES

682 If the dishwasher doesn't fill, first be sure the water is turned on. Then check to see if the float is dirty, stuck, or out of position. If the float seems stuck, remove it, check for any obstructions, and replace it. If the float isn't the problem, see if the inlet valve screen is clogged. (Check your user's manual for the location of these parts.)

683 If the dishwasher doesn't drain properly, check for a clogged strainer, pump, or drain valve. Make sure the hose is not kinked.

684 If dishes don't come out clean, check the water temperature by turning on the hot-water faucet closest to the dishwasher. Hold a cooking thermometer under the flow. If the temperature is lower than that recommended by the dishwasher manufacturer, consider turning up your water heater's thermostat. Many newer dishwashers have preheaters that boost the temperature of incoming water, regardless of your water heater's setting. Other causes for poor cleaning include a clogged strainer, sprayer, or detergent dispenser, and old, lumpy detergent that doesn't dissolve properly.

685 If the dishwasher leaks or overflows, check the door gasket; it may be damaged or loose. Check, too, for a clogged inlet valve, loose hose clamp, or defective pump seal. Make sure the dishwasher is level; adjust the legs if necessary. Are you using too much detergent? Oversudsing causes leaking. Check the cutoff switch, too; it may be stuck or need replacing.

APPLIANCE SAVINGS

686 The cost of an appliance goes far beyond the sticker price. The energy you use over the life of an appliance often costs double or triple the retail price. And wasted energy creates needless pollution. A house with the most efficient appliances could save up to $5,000 over 20 years.

For example, 1993 model refrigerators consume 25 to 30 percent less than models manufactured in 1990. In fact, based on an average electricity cost of 8.25 cents per kilowatt-hour, a 1993 refrigerator costs $100 less to run per year than a 1972 model.

687 Figuring Savings

Bright yellow EnergyGuide labels displayed on most appliances list their estimated annual energy costs. The label also gives the yearly costs of operating the least and most efficient appliances in that category.

To figure the life-cycle cost, add the sticker price (for a refrigerator we've assumed a cost of $500 in the example below) to the operating cost (gas or electricity) over 20 years.

Life-Cycle Costs

Most efficient model	Least efficient model
Original price................. $500	Original price................. $500
Energy use................. $1,700	Energy use................. $2,580
($85 x 20 years)	($129 x 20 years)
Total.......................... $2,200	Total.......................... $3,080

688 The total life-cycle savings is $880. Multiply savings like these by the number of appliances in your house and the total could be enough to help pay for a vacation, furnish a room, or send a child to college (depending on where they go). To fine-tune your equations, check with your utility company for the energy costs in your area and compare those with the chart on the EnergyGuide label on the appliance.

Reduce Pollution

689 On the average, nationally, appliances account for about 28 pounds of carbon dioxide for every dollar you spend on electricity (generated by coal or oil) and about 20 pounds of carbon dioxide for every dollar of natural gas. With these figures and the EnergyGuide label, you can assess how much pollution you can prevent with efficient appliances. In the example above, the $44 a year difference between high- and low-efficiency models adds up to 1,232 pounds ($44 x 28 pounds) of carbon dioxide every year.

APPLIANCE SHINE-UP

690 Refrigerator/Freezer
Appliance companies recommend that you unplug the refrigerator or freezer before washing the interior. Wash the exterior and interior, including the removable shelves and drawers, with warm, soapy water or use warm water with baking soda added (about 2 tablespoons per quart). Rinse thoroughly and dry. When cleaning glass shelves, let the glass warm up to room temperature before immersing the shelves in warm (not hot) water.

691 Once or twice a year, use a vacuum cleaner or a long-handled bottle brush to clean dust and lint from the condenser coils located behind the toe grille or on the back of the refrigerator. Lint and dust act as insulation, trapping heat and preventing the coils from working properly. Also, remove the drain pan, usually behind the toe grille, and wash it in soapy water.

692 Clean the door gaskets (the rubber lining around the edge of the refrigerator and freezer doors) with soapy water once or twice a year. At the same time, to keep the gaskets pliable, rub the flat edge of the gaskets with a light coating of petroleum jelly, wiping off the excess.

693 Dishwasher Clean the control panel with a slightly damp cloth. Avoid using abrasive cleansers, scrapers, or scouring pads. Clean the outside with appliance wax or a damp cloth. Because the finish can scratch, avoid abrasives. With a damp cloth, clean regularly around the door seal where food particles get caught.

694 The inside of your dishwasher should clean itself; however, if it does need cleaning, use a mild cleanser. If you notice a white powdery coating on the interior, a rotten egg smell, or a rusty discoloration, consult your user's manual. Your water could be the problem.

695 Microwave Oven Wipe the interior and exterior regularly, including the control panel, with a cloth or sponge dampened with warm sudsy water. For tough-to-remove spatters, place a cup of water in the oven. Bring the water to boiling, then, with a damp cloth, wipe over the interior of the oven.

696 Range and Oven
Wash, rinse, and dry the exterior (including stainless steel trim) regularly with a mild detergent. Clean glass parts, such as a control panel or an oven-door window, with glass cleaner and a lint-free cloth. Most control buttons and dials can be removed for easier cleaning. Wash with hot, soapy water. Between major cleanings, wash a cool oven interior with mild detergent and water, rinsing thoroughly.

Wipe up spills from the range while the surface is still warm. Do not clean the bake or broil elements. Spilled food will burn off when these elements are heated.

OUR ENVIRONMENT
ENERGY, POLLUTION, AND YOUR APPLIANCES

697 Refrigerators
Refrigerators with the freezer on top are more efficient than side-by-side models. The most efficient sizes are in the 15- to 20-cubic-foot range.

698 Dishwashers Automatic dishwashers use less water than washing by hand—as little as 6 gallons versus about 16 gallons per load. Look for models that have several wash levels and features such as rinse-and-hold and air-dry cycles. Consider, too, a booster heater, which produces the 140-degree water you need for hygiene without raising the setting on your water heater.

699 Washing machines
Front-load washing machines use a third less water than top-load models. Some 90 percent of the energy used to wash clothes is spent to heat the water, so match the clothes volume to the water levels carefully.

700 Dryers The most advanced models of clothes dryers have moisture meters that stop the machine when the clothes are sufficiently dry. And nothing beats the energy efficiency of a solar clothes dryer—hanging the wash out on a clothesline to dry in the sun.

701 Cooking Convection ovens cook food faster and at lower temperatures making them up to 40 percent more efficient than conventional ovens. Microwave ovens can be as much as two-thirds more efficient than conventional ovens especially when heating small portions. Most new ranges today have electric ignition rather than a constantly burning pilot light—a good reason for getting rid of an old gas pilot-light range.

GIVE YOUR CABINETS A FACELIFT WITH GLASS

702 Before you dig into a cabinet face-lift, make sure your cabinetry is fit for glass fronts. Almost all cabinets, except metal ones, are candidates. You can add glass to flat plywood fronts. You can also cut openings for glass in cabinets with raised panels. Just make sure the cabinets are sturdy enough to support the weight of the glass, and make any repairs if joints on the cabinet fronts are separating.

703 Consider, too, how much the makeover will cost. If you're planning to repaint, you'll spend only a few dollars for a fresh look. If you're planning on new hardware and some other trims, consider your options carefully. After all, it's easy to spend $4 or more per knob. If your cabinetry is in bad shape, it may not be wise to spend more than the cost of new paint.

If you decide to go ahead with the makeover, make sure you carefully prepare your cabinet doors before adding a new finish.

704 Remove doors from the cabinet boxes and remove the cabinet hardware. If you're changing hardware, fill the old screw holes and sand smooth.

705 Make any major repairs such as regluing loose parts. Fill holes with surfacing compound or caulk; fill gaps where wood pieces have shrunk.

706 How's the finish? It may be worthwhile to strip the old finish to get a smooth base for the new look or sand rough spots before you resurface. There are solvents that take the place of sanding. Read the label to decide whether these products will work for you.

707 If the surface of the cabinets is smooth and doesn't require any repairs, scrub the cabinets with a heavy-duty powder cleaner. Liquid cleaners can leave a film on the surface that interferes with paint adhesion.

708 For painted finishes, coat the surface with a good-quality primer.

STRETCH KITCHEN SPACE

Any kitchen needs to be planned well to get the most out of the space available but this is especially true if your kitchen is small. Consider these tips to stretch kitchen space by planning well for storage.

709 Glass used in upper-cabinet doors lets the eye see through a solid surface and creates the illusion of added space.

710 Put the space between upper and base cabinets to good use. Six-inch-deep storage niches will keep paper towels, coffee cups, spices, or a recipe box within easy reach. (Measure the things you want to store and tailor each bin to size.)

711 Planning for a peninsula instead of a wall gives a more open feeling, and adds storage and counter space.

712 Create an illusion of space with open shelves instead of upper cabinets.

713 Pullout cutting boards supplement counter space and can be used as a dining space for one.

714 Install a flip-up section at the end of a counter to increase work space.

715 Bump out an appliance niche, with an electrical outlet.

Putting the sink in a corner makes good use of an often-wasted space, yet allows work stations at each side and takes advantage of the space-enhancing window.

BONUS TRAY STORAGE

Store hard-to-fit serving trays vertically in a custom-built space beside the refrigerator.

BONUS BUILD A LID DRAWER

Tired of rummaging through drawers to find the right-size pot lid? This customized drawer solves that problem and expands storage space by organizing all those lids in one easy-to-reach spot.

HOW TO PAINT A GREAT FINISH

Follow these tips for a painted finish you'll be proud to show off.

716 Washing a surface before painting is often more important than applying two coats. A light scrubbing with soap and water removes most problems. For mold and mildew, add about 1 quart of household bleach to 3 quarts of water.

717 Don't paint over a wet surface. To hold the paint effectively, the surface should be clean, smooth, and dry. If the weather is making the walls wet inside or out, run an air conditioner or dehumidifier or wait for better conditions before you paint.

718 Avoid exposing the fresh paint to direct sunlight which causes bubbling, cracking, and other problems.

719 Apply two thin coats instead of one thick layer of paint. Even if small blemishes show through a thin first coat, resist the temptation to load on extra paint. A single thick layer is likely to dry unevenly and leave lap marks.

720 QUICK-AND-EASY RECYCLING CENTER

Make clever use of under-sink cabinet space by installing a convenient recycling center. This project requires only a handsaw and screwdriver, $75 to $150 in hardware, and a few hours.

may need to use two short baskets, or place a bigger basket in an adjacent cabinet. Carefully align the tracks for the baskets, and attach the tracks to the base of the cabinets with screws. Drop in the baskets and you're on your way to hassle-free recycling.

STEP 2: Install the basket tracks. Include an inch for clearance between baskets and between the baskets and the doors. Check operation before you tighten the screws.

The rolling wire baskets cost $25 to $50 each. To determine width, measure your cabinet from the inside surface of one door to the inside surface of the other. For clearance, give yourself at least an inch between the baskets and an inch between the baskets and the doors.

The drainpipes for most sinks come down to within 8 to 12 inches of the floor of the cabinet. In the middle, we used a basket that is just 6 inches tall. It has adequate clearance and easily stores a week's worth of newspapers. If you have a garbage disposal, you

STEP 1: Cut out the center stile between the doors of your sink cabinet. The stile is not a structural support. It only serves to provide a seal to close the gap between the two doors. Next, screw and glue the stile to the back of one of the doors. Allow the stile to extend beyond the edge of the door so that when both doors are closed, the stile seals the gap. If your doors have lips, cut a matching lip on the stile before attaching it to the door.

STEP 3: Drop in the baskets. To clear the sink drain or garbage disposal, you may need to use one or two shorter baskets. Note the stile attached to the back of the cabinet door.

THE LAUNDRY

LAUNDRY REQUIREMENTS

721 Utility connections: An automatic washer requires a drain and plumbing lines for both hot and cold water. The washer needs a 115-volt, 60Hz electrical outlet and should have its own circuit. An electric dryer requires its own 230-volt, 60Hz, three-wire circuit. A gas dryer requires a gas-supply line and a 115-volt, 60Hz connection for the motor. This outlet should be on a separate circuit from the washer. All laundry appliances should be properly grounded.

722 Venting the dryer: All standard clothes dryers, gas or electric, should be vented to the outdoors.

723 A SPACE-EFFICIENT LAUNDRY CENTER

Hidden behind folding doors are a stacked washer and dryer, 4½ linear feet of well-lit counter space, a built-in hamper, shelves, and a cubby for the ironing board.

MONEY $ MATTERS
LOWERING LAUNDRY UTILITY COSTS

BONUS Save energy and money by setting your water heater at 140 degrees Fahrenheit for laundry use.

BONUS Switch to a cold rinse for every load. It's just as effective as a warm rinse.

BONUS Try to dry laundry in consecutive loads. Otherwise you are wasting the energy used to bring the dryer up to the desired temperature.

BONUS Keep the lint filter clean. A buildup of lint on the filter restricts airflow and requires the dryer to run longer than necessary to dry clothes. A clean filter also helps reduce the need for service calls.

724 COMMONSENSE PLACEMENT

Stop hauling clothes back and forth to the basement. Make laundry equipment more accessible by locating it near the bedroom or bathroom, where dirty clothes are generated. Another handy site is in a closet or hall near the kitchen, so you can do laundry as you do other kitchen tasks.

BATHS: DESIGN

ENHANCE SPACE

Use these tricks to make a small bath feel bigger.

725 Push out a wall with light. Shadowy corners shrink a room. Illuminate those areas with wall fixtures or track lights.

726 Bring in more natural light by replacing a tiny window above the tub with a large garden window or glass block. Skylights are another good option.

727 Replace space-stealing fixtures with sleeker alternatives—trade a bulky vanity for a pedestal sink.

728 Think vertical. Direct the eye upward with wood moldings, borders, and vertical stripes.

729 For those who love to soak, trade a standard-size tub for a deep, but small-circumference soaking tub. Or, remove the tub and install a corner shower.

730 Eliminate clutter. Sweep countertops clean. Keep wallpapers light and smaller scale. Avoid frilly curtains or furry bath mats.

731 Stick with one finish, such as tile, on as many surfaces as possible.

732 Use mirrors to make your bath look larger.

MONEY $ MATTERS

CUT COSTS

These ideas can help you put your dollars where your dream is:

733 Cut costs by doing much of the labor yourself but avoid costly mistakes by getting professional design advice. Many designers will work on a per-hour basis.

734 Limit relocating fixtures especially the toilet. You might want to first consider pointing a fixture in a different direction or sliding the sink into a corner. If your bathroom just won't work without moving a fixture, then it's worth the expense to get the function you need.

735 Shop for bargains. Be willing to search through "seconds" at home centers and plumbing suppliers to find that near-perfect fixture. Watch ads for sales. Keep an eye on the classified ads for new materials left over from a large remodeling.

736 Keep your color palette white. White fixtures—tubs, toilets, and sinks—cost less than those in colors.

737 Ask for discounts. If you're remodeling more than one bathroom, many stores are willing to cut a deal in order to gain all of your business.

738 Buy look-alike laminates for expensive materials such as marble and granite. Also choose plain tiles and create your own pattern with two or three colors. Or select just a few hand-painted tiles to sprinkle in with plain tiles.

739 ADD STORAGE

There are several ways to help a small bathroom store more. Equip a vanity with space organizers so you can make good use of the available space.

You don't need more than four inches of depth to store anything in the bathroom. Use the space between studs, for example to create a shallow 16-inch-wide cabinet that's 6 feet tall. By doing so, you're really providing an incredible amount of storage. It's very handy because then all those things aren't lost in the back of a vanity cabinet. Make the door to your stud cabinet vanish by having it double as a full-length mirror set flush with a surrounding mirrored wall.

If your bathroom is wider than 5 feet, you may have space at the foot of the tub for installing shelving or a cabinet. You also may want to consider hanging shallow shelves on the back of your bathroom entry door or above the toilet.

For additional counter space, stretch your countertop material from the vanity across the top of the toilet.

MINIMUM CLEARANCES

740 Provide a clear walkway of at least 32 inches at all bathroom entrances.

741 Allow at least 21 inches of walkway space in front of the sink, the tub/shower, and the toilet.

742 Ensure a minimum clearance of 12 inches from the center of the sink to any side wall.

743 Provide a minimum clearance of 30 inches from the center of one sink to the center of another.

744 Allow at least 15 inches from the center of the toilet to any obstruction, fixture, or equipment on either side.

745 Allow a 6-inch clearance for cleaning between fixtures.

746 Provide a shower interior of at least 32 inches square.

747 Make sure the shower door swings into the bathroom.

SAFETY

No matter how serene your new bath looks or how smoothly it functions, there is plenty of potential for accidents. Observe these precautions:

748 Use only slip-resistant flooring. Purchase new showers or tubs with a slip-resistant floor. If your tub or shower is old, add nonslip strips to the floor.

749 Install ground-fault circuit interrupters (GFCI) on all outlets. A GFCI stops the flow of electricity if it senses any leakage of current. All lights above tub-shower units should be moisture-proof, special-purpose fixtures.

750 Keep glass out of the bathroom. Shower doors should be tempered safety glass or acrylic only. Use plastic or paper cups for drinking.

751 To prevent scalds, install a temperature-limiting device on all faucets.

752 Avoid sharp edges. Choose rounded corners on countertops and other bathroom components.

753 Be sure to install lighting over the bathtub or shower as well as over the mirror. Adequate lighting goes a long way in preventing cuts from shaving and other accidents.

LIGHT IT RIGHT

To supplement natural light, consider these points:

754 In medium or large baths, a ceiling fixture centered over the front edge of the sink is a necessity.

755 Light a vanity mirror from each side or from both sides and top. Install side fixtures 28 to 36 inches apart and centered 60 inches above the floor. If you're using incandescent light, you need at least one 75-watt or two 40- to 60-watt bulbs on each side.

756 Each side of theatrical or strip lighting should have four to six globe-shape bulbs.

757 For fluorescent light, install a 24-inch, 20-watt tube on each side and possibly one above the mirror.

USER-FRIENDLY DESIGN

These concepts of universal design make a bathroom safe and accessible to anyone regardless of age, size, or ability.

758 A bench or drop-down shower seat helps the elderly shower safely and it's great for washing or shaving legs.

759 A shower head on a slide bar adjusts for use by people of any height, even seated.

760 Lever-style door and faucet handles work best.

761 Use drawers or retractable doors in base cabinets and wire pulls instead of knobs.

762 A built-in step stool under the vanity helps kids reach the sink.

763 Install outlets and light switches no more than 54 inches off the floor.

764 Choose a slip-resistant flooring material.

765 Electrical outlets near a water source should be placed on a ground fault circuit interrupter (GFCI) which instantly shuts off the flow of electricity of current leaks.

766 Consider installing grab bars above the tub and in the shower stall.

767 The standard vanity stands at 32 inches. For many people, that height is too low for comfort. Experts recommend that the rim of the sink be 34 to 38 inches from the floor.

SAVVY REMODELING STRATEGIES

768 A quality exhaust fan should be a priority in any bath remodeling. With a duct to the outside, a fan removes moisture, odors, and aerosol pollutants.

769 Before you make remodeling decisions that involve moving fixtures, remember that moving fixtures can throw your budget way out of whack. Relocating the toilet, for example, can be expensive. Toilets must stay within a few feet of the stack, the vertical pipe that carries waste to the main drain. A new stack will be necessary if you move the toilet—a costly proposition.

770 Does your household have too many people and not enough baths? Why not add a small grooming station (a vanity, sink, and mirror) in a bedroom. This is actually economical if the bedroom is adjacent to a bath, laundry, or the kitchen and if the plumbing pipes run through the shared wall.

771 Select surfacing materials on the basis of durability. The water and steam in a bath take a toll on products such as wallpaper, carpeting, and wood flooring. Alkyd (resin-based) paint is the most durable wall finish, but vinyl-type wallcoverings will hold up in a bathroom that is well vented. Ceramic tile and vinyl are your best bets for the floor.

EASY TO CLEAN SURFACES

772 Avoid light-colored grout, particularly around the shower. The grout is just about impossible to keep clean and its uneven surface makes it an ideal home for mold and mildew.

773 A complete tub-shower unit has no seams, making it easier to clean. Solid-surface surrounds are also seamless and, while they're more expensive than fiberglass, they look and feel more substantial.

774 Treat yourself to a good-size linen closet or build shelves in the bath.

775 In the great debate over shower doors versus curtains most home economists agree that curtains are easier to care for. Simply toss them in the wash with a few towels. But if you must have doors on your shower, invest in a good, sturdy set and keep a squeegee on hand to clean them after each shower.

776 HOW MUCH SPACE IS ENOUGH?

For a half bath (sink and toilet) you'll need at least 4 feet by 4 feet 8 inches or 6 feet 8 inches by 2 feet 8 inches. A three-quarter bath (sink, toilet, and shower stall) will fit a nook as small as 6 feet by 6 feet. The minimum size for a full bath is 5 feet by 7 feet.

MAKE YOUR MASTER BATH WORK FOR TWO

777 Which spouse gets to bathe or shower first? Eliminate any competition by separating the shower and tub. Another option is to build a roomy shower enclosure and install two shower heads.

778 Avoid knocking elbows at the sink by building two vanities or by building a long vanity with two sinks.

779 Customize fixtures to the user's height. If you and your spouse stand at very different heights, buy a shower head that slides vertically on a rod, letting users adjust the height as necessary. If one spouse is tall, raise the vanity to a height of 34 to 36 inches rather than the standard 32 inches. (If you're buying a stock vanity cabinet, look instead at kitchen base units that stand 36 inches tall.)

780 To maximize privacy, install the toilet in a separate compartment. To save space, use a pocket door—one that slides into an interior wall—rather than a swinging door.

PROJECT PRIMER

BONUS **REPLACING CERAMIC TILE**

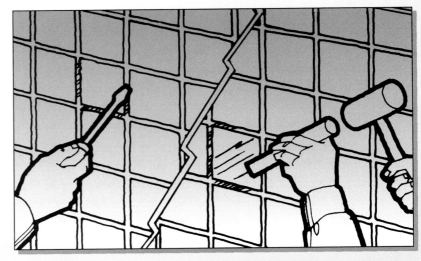

Ceramic tile is a durable wall treatment for a bathroom. Occasionally, however, one or more tiles need to be replaced because settling causes the tile to crack or permanent stains leave unsightly blots on the wall.

To make repairs, isolate the damaged tiles by chipping away the grout, *above,* then smash the tiles and knock out the pieces. Scrape any old adhesive from the wall. To replace a few tiles, spread a thin coat of adhesive on the tiles; for a large area, spread the adhesive on the wall. Press the tile into place, then pound with your fist to fix the adhesive. Wipe excess adhesive from the surface. Mix grout to the consistency of a thick paste and apply it

with diagonal passes of a rubber float, *above,* taking care to pack all joints. After 15 minutes, smooth the joints with a rounded object, such as the handle of a toothbrush. Clean off excess grout on the tile with a wet sponge and polish with a dry cloth.

MIRROR, MIRROR...

781 Mirroring walls is a great way to add dimension to a small space. To have sheet mirrors like these installed in a bath, you'll probably want to work with a glass specialty company. The company will precut the mirror to your dimensions and deliver and mount it. For installation, workers affix a special channel to the base of your wall, snug the mirror in, and adhere the glass to the wall with mastic. You may not need the channel if the mirror can rest on baseboards.

782 You can mount sconce lights, towel bars, and accessories over the mirror as long as there are precut holes. Some suppliers will cut the openings on site. Openings can also be cut for mirrored medicine cabinets.

783 Expect to pay $6 to $8 per square foot for a simple sheet mirror, installed, plus $5 to $30 for each hole cut. Tricky angles or seam strips will cost extra.

784 GLASS BLOCKS

They admit light yet preserve privacy. Glass blocks create wonderful grid patterns anywhere but they're especially useful in a bathroom. Installed, glass block runs about $25 per square foot. Do-it-yourselfers will find the average 6-inch-square block costs from $3 to $4. Curved or angled corner blocks and curved end blocks are available as are several different shapes, patterns, and sizes. The weight of glass block can be a concern. You may need extra floor supports if your glass-block wall does not rest on a bearing wall or concrete slab.

BATHS:
SHOWERS AND TUBS

785 MAKE A MUSLIN SHOWER CURTAIN

You can make a classy shower curtain from cotton muslin—a material that comes in a variety of widths, finishes, and prices. Untreated cotton muslin can cost less than $1 per yard, but it wrinkles after washing. For good cotton muslin with a permanent-press finish you'll pay about $4 per yard, depending on the fabric width.

To figure how much fabric you'll need measure the width of the space; double that for fullness. To make the fabric puddle on the floor add to the length.

Cut the material to size, allowing for seams, turned-under edges, a deep facing at the top edge, and a hem along the bottom of the curtain. Seam the pieces; press flat. Turn under vertical edges. To make the top edge, attach fabric tabs, then sew a facing piece over the edge. Turn the fabric right side out and slip the tabs over a rod. Or punch grommets all along the top edge to accept shower-curtain hooks. To finish, pair your curtain with a vinyl shower-curtain liner.

786 RECAULKING YOUR SHOWER

Sooner or later every shower will need its corner and tub seams recaulked. Tackle the job as soon as cracks appear and it will cost only about $3 in caulk and 20 minutes of your time. Wait until dry rot sets in and the repair bill could be hundreds of dollars.

Cracks in the seams of your shower occur from the regular expansion and contraction of walls due to changes in temperature and humidity. Tub seams are even more vulnerable because most tubs flex when you step into them. Recaulking with a silicone or water-based caulk provides the best long-term protection. These products are long lasting and highly elastic. If you are doing only one shower, a 2.8-fluid-ounce tube is quicker and easier to handle than a cartridge in a caulking gun.

STEP 1: Prepare the shower. Clean all soap residue and mildew from the walls. Use a knife to dig the old caulk from corners and tub seams.

STEP 2: Apply the caulk. Cut the applicator tip so that the opening is 1/8 inch in diameter. Apply a continuous line about 3 feet long.

STEP 3: Smooth the line. Silicone becomes tacky fast, so smooth the first line with your finger as soon as you lay it. If

the caulk should flow around the sides of your finger, immediately wipe away the excess with a soft cloth. Use

warm, soapy water and your finger to re-form the joint. Wait at least 12 hours before using the shower.

787 CONSIDER WEIGHT

Before making plans to install any type of tub, make sure your floor joists can hold the weight. A standard 5-foot iron tub, for example, tips the scales at about 500 pounds; a 6-foot tub, up to 700 pounds. If you put in 50 gallons of water and add a 200-pound adult, the total is a hefty 1,100 to 1,300 pounds—more than a half-ton.

Some manufacturers produce models in lightweight acrylic—ideal for second-floor remodeling projects—but it's wise to consult a professional before installing any tub.

SAFETY CHECK

The most common accidents in the bath include falling or slipping while getting in or out of a tub. Avoid mishaps with these safety precautions:

788 Install slip-resistant flooring around the tub.

789 Make sure the faucet controls are easy to reach from both inside and outside the tub.

790 Forgo a sunken tub for one accessed by steps. Each riser should be at most 7 inches high, and each tread should be at least 10 inches deep. Allow enough room to sit on the edge and swing your legs over the edge.

GOOD MEASURES

Standard rectangular tubs measure 54, 60, or 72 inches long, 32 to 40 inches wide, and 12 to 20 inches deep. Other dimensions to keep in mind:

791 The minimum size of a full bath is 5x7 feet.

792 There should be a walkway clearance of 21 to 30 inches between the tub and the wall or fixture opposite it.

793 For comfort, a tub for two should be 42 inches wide.

794 DON'T CRACK THE CAULK

Before applying caulk between your bathtub and the wall, be sure to fill the tub with water. The water will expand the tub. This will keep the caulk from cracking because of the tub's movement.

795 FIGHT CAULK STAINS

Use rubbing alcohol to remove mildew and other stains from the silicone caulking around your tub.

BONUS NO-SCUM SHOWER DOORS

Having trouble ridding your glass shower doors of film and scum? Rub the doors with mineral oil to create clear and shiny glass.

BATHS:
TOILETS AND SINKS

796 UNDERSTANDING YOUR TOILET

Repairing a problem toilet isn't anyone's idea of a good time but you'll have to do it every so often nonetheless. Most toilet maladies happen inside the tank where all the mechanical parts are. Only rarely will other problems develop.

Lift the top off the toilet tank and you'll find—mostly submerged in water—an assortment of balls, tubes, and levers similar to those illustrated at *right.* To understand what they do, first realize that flipping the handle sets in motion a chain of events that releases water to the bowl, then automatically refills both the tank and the bowl.

In the flushing cycle, moving the handle activates a trip lever that lifts a flush ball at the bottom of the tank. Water then rushes through a seat into the toilet. After the tank empties, the flush ball drops back into its seat.

Flushing also triggers the refill cycle thanks to a float ball that goes down along with the water level and opens an inlet valve. This brings fresh water into the tank via a refill tube; it also sends water to the bowl through a second refill tube that empties into an overflow tube.

As the water rises, so does the float ball. When it reaches a point ¾ inch or so below the top of the overflow, the float shuts off the inlet valve.

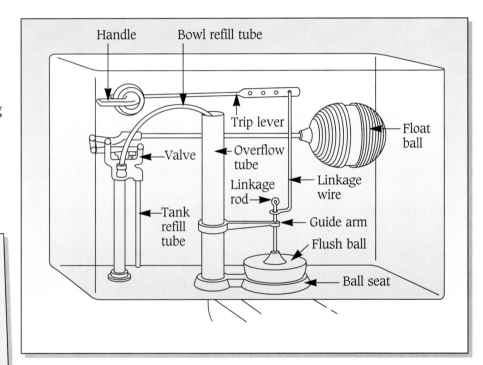

BONUS MEASURING FOR FAUCET REPLACEMENT

Most sinks are predrilled at standard distances to fit a faucet's supply pipes. To replace a faucet, measure from the outside edge of one pipe to the inside edge of the other. For example, if this measurement is 4 inches, the faucet is classified as "4 inches, on center."

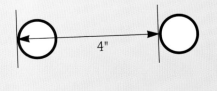

4"

BONUS FITTING A FAUCET

Before you purchase any faucet, make sure it fits your sink. Handles should align with the predrilled holes in the deck of the sink; the spout should extend over the bowl but not block it.

TROUBLESHOOTING TOILETS

PROBLEM	SOLUTION
Toilet won't flush	**797** Check the handle, trip lever, guide arm, float arm, and the connections between each one of the parts to make sure all are functioning. The handle may be too loose or tight, the trip lever or guide arm may be bent or broken, the connection between the trip lever and guide arm may be broken or out of adjustment so it doesn't raise the flush ball far enough.
Water runs, but tank won't fill properly	**798** The handle and trip assembly may be malfunctioning. See above. Check the flush ball for proper seating, check the seat for corrosion, and check the float for water inside.
Water runs constantly after the tank is filled	**799** You may have to adjust the float downward. Check the float to make sure it's not damaged. It could be full of water causing it to float improperly. The inlet valve washers may be leaking and need replacement. Check to see that the flush ball is seating properly. Check the ball seat for corrosion.
The water level is set too high or too low	**800** Gently bend the float arm downward to lower the water level. Bend it upward to raise the water level. Or, use the adjustment screw on top of the inlet valve to set the float arm. The water should be ¾ inch below the top of the overflow tube. Some inlet valves are shut off by a cylindrical float around the inlet valve attached to the top of the valve by a thin metal rod. You can adjust these floats by pinching a small clamp on the side of the float and moving the float up or down to raise or lower the water level.
Toilet won't flush properly	**801** Water may be too low in the tank. If so, bend the float ball arm up to permit sufficient water to flow into the toilet bowl. Or, if you have a cylindrical float, pinch the clamp on the side of the float and raise it.
Water splashes in the tank while it refills	**802** Adjust the refill tube that runs into the overflow tube. You may need to replace the washers in the inlet valve.
Tank leaks at the bottom	**803** Tighten the nuts at the bottom of the tank but be careful. Just snugging the nuts up should do the trick. If you overtighten the nuts you run the risk of cracking the toilet. If this doesn't work, replace the washers.

DECORATING
OLD INTO NEW

804 DIVIDER DOORS

Hinge together a quartet of mismatched doors and salvaged sidelights, creating a room screen that visually divides a room but still lets in the sun. For best results, choose doors and sidelights that are similar in height, width, and color. The ones shown *below,* for example, are all tall and narrow with light paint or wood and lots of open spaces. Pick whatever doors fit your space then join them with cabinet hinges, making sure the bottoms are even.

805 RECIPE FOR A KITCHEN TABLE

To make a worktable like the one *at right,* you'll need a few basic supplies from your local lumberyard as well as a slab of marble or other material to form the tabletop.

To make the frame, butt-join 1x8s. Make the base of the table a few inches smaller than the diameter of the marble top so the top extends beyond the frame. Brace the frame with cross-struts. Screw pressure-treated porch posts (found at the lumberyard) into each corner of the frame to serve as legs. Stain, paint, or polish the table base as desired, then set the marble in place atop the frame.

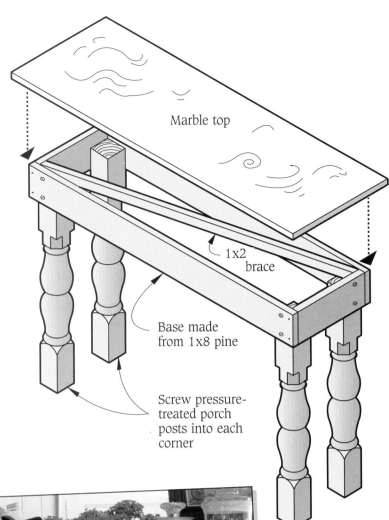

Marble top

1x2 brace

Base made from 1x8 pine

Screw pressure-treated porch posts into each corner

806 RURAL SHELF

Add a touch of rustic Americana with a wall-hung shelf formed from clean-lined corbels and weathered barn board. Even though these brackets appear to be supporting the shelf, the barn wood really does the work. Construct the shelf and apron (the part of the shelf that is against the wall and at a right angle to the shelf top) from solid barn wood or other rustic planks. Attach the corbels for decoration.

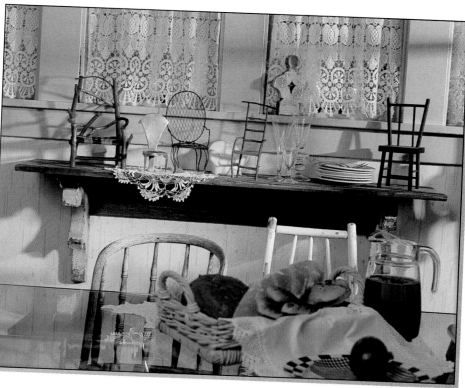

807 DOORKNOB HANGERS

Hang your duds high on a hodgepodge of ornate doorknobs. Cut dowels to fit the shank of each knob, leaving some dowel to extend into, but not through, the base. Spacing the knobs evenly, drill holes in the base to receive each dowel. Mount the board on the wall at two holes. Glue the dowels in place; screw the knobs to the dowels.

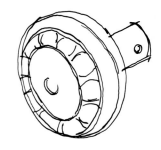

COLOR TRICKS

Color is the great deceiver and by using the right hues to create illusions you can visually remodel an awkward room or personalize a space with special effects. Here are some suggestions for working design magic with color.

808 In a small room, the space-expanding prescription is to unite walls and ceiling in a sweep of white or light color. Carry the light hue to the floor with neutral carpet.

809 Square up a long, narrow room by painting walls in advancing and receding colors. For example, use a warm, dark hue on short end walls to coax them forward, then use a white or light hue on long side walls to diminish their importance.

810 Tame a too-high ceiling by painting it in an advancing color such as brown or dark blue that seemingly brings it down. Enhance the effect by extending the dark color down the wall to a picture molding or other natural demarcation line.

811 Make a too-low ceiling seem higher with a receding color such as white or a pastel.

812 Disguise a room's flaws with color magic. If walls are broken up by doorways, windows, and various nooks and crannies, paint away such interruptions with a light or white wall color applied over frames and all. You can even make an unsightly feature such as an old fireplace almost disappear by painting it the same color as the walls.

A variety of prints, stripes, and textures work well in this room because they are unified by color.

PUTTING PATTERNS IN THEIR PLACE

Mixing and matching patterns and prints can create visual interest or an optical disaster. When choosing the fabric and wallpapers for a room, keep these guidelines in mind.

813 Don't Overdo It
Too many patterns or prints can confuse the eye; therefore, limit your choices to a few special designs. A stripe will coordinate with almost any pattern and can give the eye a more interesting place to rest than on a solid.

814 Unify By Color
One easy way to mix patterns is to choose them by color. Florals, stripes, geometrics, and other motifs look like family when they share even a small amount of hue.

815 Consider Scale
Patterns and prints should complement the scale of the room or the piece of furniture. Petite designs work well on pillows, dust ruffles, or small windows. Large patterns are better suited to walls, bedspreads, draperies, or sofas.

Scale should also vary within a room. Too many large patterns will fight with each other; too many small prints will lack a focal point.

816 Follow a Formula
Still baffled? Follow this formula: Mix one large-scale print, a medium stripe, and a small light print. Or choose patterns from the same matched collection. For reassurance, tack samples on the walls and furniture to see if they work together.

133

FINISHING TOUCHES

Your sofa is in place, the chair looks inviting, and the lamp is plugged in. Still, something is missing. Could it be that you stopped decorating too soon? Consider the extra touches that fill in a room's blanks with instant personality.

Before

After

817 Gather objects of affection in a close-knit group. Inherited family furnishings, such as the table and rocker shown here, join hands with a friendly screen made from antique doors. Together, they corner some privacy in a room. Touch up your own similar arrangements with a pair of antique prints, tabletop treats (note the pretty peach potpourri and majolica), and an antique tapestry pillow.

818 Go to great panes with fabrics. What a difference a decorating day makes. Yesterday this bare-bones window seat invited no sitters. Today, with a light-filtering fabric shade, a lyrical valance, and soft, cushioned seating, it offers a cozy nook for reading and a side table for tea and trinkets.

After

Before

819 Give barren walls gallery glory. You may have the antidote for ho-hum walls hiding in albums or scattered about in old frames, unnoticed. Invite cherished family photos to a reunion, turning that blah spot into one that evokes a smile. For impact, outline loved ones with crisp, new frames.

After

Before

ROOM ARRANGING

Certain rooms exude natural grace and a feeling of comfort. Their inviting arrangements draw us in, coaxing us to stay awhile. Such rooms spring from timeless decorating principles that have long guided room-shapers. For gracious rooms of your own, take these rules to heart and home.

820 Begin with function. Decide how you plan to use the room, listing the activities you and your family would like to do there. Feel free to change room labels and use your space creatively. Who says that your dining area can't function as an office or entertainment center? Why not dine in the living room or in the guest room just off the kitchen? Look at your furnishings to see what new pieces you need and which ones should be traded away or shuffled to another room.

821 Find a focal point. A room's focus works as a cornerstone on which you build your arrangement of furnishings. It has become a magnetic element that catches the eye and draws you into a room. If your room doesn't have a natural focal point such as windows with a great view, a bookcase wall, or a fireplace, substitute a large-scale or bold-colored furniture piece or accessory. Or group small elements—a wood folding screen, a distinctive chair, and a basket of dried blooms—into a welcoming focal point.

822 Float furnishings. A lineup of furniture around the edges of a room creates an awkward "waiting room" that's anything but welcoming. To set up furniture arrangements that invite conversation, pull pieces away from the walls, gathering them into warm, close-knit groupings. If you place major seating pieces no more than about 8 feet apart, you'll never have to shout across the room.

823 Direct traffic. Although traffic passes through a room it doesn't have to travel through the center of it. Think of furniture as curbs that funnel traffic around conversation groupings. Allow a width of 2 to 3 feet for traffic lanes and for pullout space behind dining chairs. You can narrow some pathways such as the area between a sofa and a cocktail table to about 18 inches wide.

824 Do a balancing act. Combine furnishings of different heights and hefts for interest but avoid placing all of your tall or weighty pieces on the same side of the room. Use weighty pieces to balance architectural features. For instance, echo the height of a tall window or fireplace on one side of the room by placing an armoire or bookcase on the other. Or, if you have a large piano on one end of the room, balance it with a conversational seating arrangement on the other end.

825 Try a fresh angle. Because a diagonal is the longest line through any room, a grouping placed at an angle can open up space creating an illusion of width. An on-the-bias gathering can also help you take advantage of two focal points. For example, angle a sofa so you can enjoy a fireplace on one wall and a great view on the adjacent one.

826 Think convenience. Put a spot for drinks or books close to every seating piece. This can be a true end table, a stack of books, or a glass-topped basket—just be sure it's roughly the same height as the arm of your seating piece.

WORKING WITH AN INTERIOR DESIGNER

Working with an interior designer should be exciting and mutually rewarding but misunderstandings sometimes hamper the relationship. Here are five common myths or misconceptions with suggestions on how to avoid them.

MYTH #1: Interior designers never stick to a budget.

827 SOLUTION: Be open and honest about your budget from the beginning.

Homeowners often are reluctant to specify a budget. Sometimes they think the designer will automatically spend that amount when they might have gotten the job done for less. This causes problems because once clients see a design they love—but can't afford—they never seem satisfied with less costly designs. Provide a budget up front so the designer can show you realistic designs from the start instead of ideas that are out of your financial reach.

MYTH #2: Interior designers take forever to finish a job.

828 SOLUTION: Draw up a written contract that specifies all details of the interior design project, especially costs and the date of completion.

Discuss all facets of any project with the interior designer before work begins and set down in writing everything that's agreed upon. Usually experienced interior designers can accurately gauge how long it will take to finish a project. A written agreement will ensure it gets done on time.

MYTH #3: Interior designers always tell the clients what the finished project should look like regardless of the client's wishes.

829 SOLUTION: Take plenty of time to interview a number of designers and find one you're comfortable with.

Part of an interior designer's job is to help you understand what's most appropriate for your application. A kitchen island may be a big part of your remodeling plans but if it isn't structurally feasible, any qualified designer will tell you so.

Good designers don't set style trends or dictate what you should do in your space. They listen, try to understand your needs, and offer solutions to your particular design challenges. Every designer has his or her own style so do your research instead of selecting one at random.

Sometimes a referral from a friend, neighbor, or relative is helpful. You can also contact the ASID Client/Designer Selection Service for names of qualified interior designers.

MYTH #4: An interior designer won't understand the effect I want to achieve.

830 SOLUTION: The more precisely you describe your interior design needs the more successfully your designer will meet them.

Before you talk with a designer, explore the following questions and make notes of your answers.

• What do I expect from the completed project?

• Am I willing to be honest about my taste without fearing the designer won't like it?

• For whom is the space designed?

• What activities will the space be used for?

• Do I have a particular design style in mind?

• Are there certain features that absolutely must be incorporated into the design space?

If you've done your homework and chosen a designer you can freely talk to, you should have no problem working together. Most designers use visuals to show what they're planning to do. You also can request to visit projects the designer has done.

MYTH #5: I'll have to buy all the materials from the interior designer at a premium price.

831 SOLUTION: Discuss how the designer handles costs during the initial interview and determine whether it will work for you.

The nature and scope of design services vary from project to project. If you're uncomfortable having the designer purchase items, there are many other compensation alternatives, including:

• **Flat fee.** The designer identifies a specific sum to cover the complete range of services—from conceptual development through layouts and final installation.

• **Hourly fee.** Compensation is based on actual time spent on specific services.

• **Cost-plus fee.** The designer purchases material and services at wholesale prices.

832 CREATE A SENSE OF SPACE

Create a sense of more space in a small bedroom by keeping the wall color light and making use of the vertical plane. A striped wallpaper will make the ceiling seem higher. Try to minimize the window treatments with cheerful, outside-style awnings. An armoire is also helpful because it lends height and vertical storage.

833 WHAT TO DO WITH THE TV

Here's how to keep the television from being the focal point of the family room. Don't stick the TV in a corner—that makes it more obvious. You can put a smaller TV in an armoire, a piece of antique furniture, or a custom-built storage unit. However, it is perfectly acceptable to leave the TV visible and make it part of the family when the room is primarily used for entertainment.

MONEY $ MATTERS

MORE FOR LESS

Here's how to squeeze the most from your decorating dollar without compromising on style.

834 Buy good fabric at bargain prices. You'll find good deals at discount fabric stores and in remnant piles. Shop a lot of places, keep your eye out for anything unique, and do some traveling.

835 Invest in quality hardware and decorative trim. Money spent on solidly built curtain rods, interesting drawer pulls, and decorative tapes and fringes will pay off with a home that has one-of-a-kind appeal and the finished look a professional decorator brings.

836 Bone up on faux-finishing basics. Marbled floors, sponged walls, and painted furniture add instant pizzazz.

837 Find alternative artwork. Framed pages from magazines and books make unusual and inexpensive wall art.

838 Recycle furniture and fabric. Give old furniture a lift by changing its color or finish. Try lacquer for breathing new life into kitchen chairs, porch wicker, and dining-room chairs. Also, consider reusing drapery and furniture fabric.

BONUS PAY ATTENTION TO SCALE

Unmatched furniture styles can feel cozier than a perfectly matched set. To make an attractive mix, let size become the common denominator. Beef up small items by giving them dark colors or grouping them. Large furnishings seem to recede when wearing light colors or the same hues as the things around them.

RETHINK YOUR SPACES

839 Once upon a time, rooms were as predictable as the IRS in spring. You ate in the dining room, played in the family room, and reserved the living room for company. Today's open floor plans and do-it-all great rooms make those old roles obsolete. What's new: Choosing and arranging furniture to make any space live the way you need it to.

Take the floor plan *right* for example. At one time, the family used its modified-L floor plan in the usual way: The area

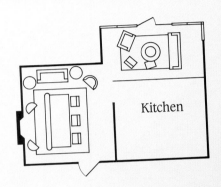

Kitchen

off the kitchen was for dining, the front room for sitting. Then they realized a better plan.

"Our guests hovered around the dining table to enjoy the sunny space and visit with the cook," the homeowner says. "Problem was, the bench was uncomfortable to sit on for long periods of time." So, the rooms traded places—shuffling the cozy seating pieces to the window-lined space and placing the harvest table in front of the hearth. Now the cook is part of the action before the meal is served and it's wonderful to eat by the fire on chilly evenings.

BONUS A crackling fire and access to the kitchen make this former living room an inviting dining spot.

BONUS After switching places with the dining room, the living room now delights in lots of sunshine.

LIGHTING FOR TIRED EYES

Beginning at about age 40, eyes have a tougher time focusing on close-up tasks, adapting to sudden changes in light intensity, and tolerating glare. Here are some bright ideas for improving the lighting around your home.

840 Eliminate excessive contrasts in lighting—bright pools of light surrounded by darkness. To do this, supplement task lights such as table or floor lamps and pendants with general, or "ambient," light from ceiling or wall fixtures, recessed or track lighting, or chandeliers.

841 Illuminate a room slowly to help your eyes make the transition from dark to light. For instance, turn on table lamps before you flick on bright overhead lighting. Use plenty of small, light-sensitive night-lights to help ease nighttime transitions around your home.

842 Avoid direct glare from unshielded fixtures such as track lights by aiming them at a wall. This way, light bounces back into the room, and you don't see the light bulb. Or use baffles or diffusers to shield the bulbs in track and recessed lights.

843 Minimize glare from direct sunlight with sun-filtering window treatments such as lace panels, translucent pleated shades, sheer curtains, and blinds. Don't place a TV or a desk in front or to the side of a window, which will direct your eyes into the light. Be sure to keep lights on while you're watching television to avoid troubling contrast.

844 Increase wattage in table lamps to illuminate eye-straining activities such as reading, sewing, and balancing the checkbook. In lamps, consider switching from standard incandescent bulbs to compact fluorescent ones that give more light while consuming less energy. Also replace standard floods or spotlights in track and recessed fixtures with brighter and longer-lasting screw-in halogen bulbs.

845 When decorating, use light, reflective colors on walls and carpets to enhance your home's lighting. Using dark colors over a large area will literally absorb your newfound light.

BONUS HANGING A CHANDELIER

People often hang chandeliers too low—a definite conversation blocker. When they're placed too high, on the other hand, lighting fixtures appear awkwardly unrelated to the furniture groupings below them. As a general rule for an 8-foot ceiling, allow 25 to 30 inches between the table surface and the bottom of the light fixture. For each additional foot of ceiling height raise your fixture 3 inches.

ELEMENTS OF STYLE

846 **Rustic Roots**
☐ Neutral hues with rusty red and golden tones
☐ Plaid and denim fabrics, hardwood flooring
☐ Twig chairs, log furniture
☐ Western and American Indian art
☐ Minimal window treatments, log or paneled walls

847 **Hot Tropics**
☐ Tropical tones such as coral, blue, green, and gold
☐ Canvas and linen fabrics, sisal flooring
☐ Wicker and rattan furniture
☐ Primitive paintings, folk art accents
☐ Stuccoed walls, shuttered windows

848 Cottage Chic
☐ Country color combinations: blue and white, red and white, yellow and white
☐ Gingham and airy floral fabrics, rag rugs
☐ Painted or pine furniture
☐ Afghans, quilts, nostalgic collectibles
☐ Lace-covered windows, beadboard walls

849 Back To Nature
☐ Earthy green and brown hues
☐ Fabrics printed with natural motifs, needlepoint rugs
☐ Furniture in natural wood finishes
☐ Topiaries and other greenery, botanical prints
☐ Wooden blinds, textured walls

850 Farmhouse Style

☐ Primary colors—can be muted
☐ Fabric—gingham checks, plaids, reproduction patterns, old textiles
☐ Cabinetry furnishings—rustic woods, such as maple, oak, and pine; simple lines; turned posts; V-joint or grooved doors; stile-and-rail flat-panel doors
☐ Walls—hand-plastered stucco, beaded wainscoting
☐ Windows—curtains gathered or pulled back
☐ Flooring—rustic wood planks, brick, quarry tile, or a wooden floor punctuated with ceramic tile insets
☐ Lighting—reproduction with recessed spots
☐ Accessories—favorite collectibles, anything rustic or Old World

FABRICS WITH NATURAL BEAUTY

For soft, lived-in texture, select natural fabrics. Here's what to look for.

851 Wool is the best wearing of all natural fibers. If slight pilling bothers you, avoid lofty weaves. Wool is costly so it's often wed with nylon for affordability.

852 Although durable, linen has trouble holding color and tends to wrinkle permanently. If you don't like the rumpled, worn look, shop for neutral hues that don't show fading and a cotton blend that wrinkles less.

853 Cotton takes dye beautifully but does show its age. Look for dense weaves such as canvas and denim.

854 Made from wood pulp, rayon can be lumped with the naturals. Although it offers the best color range, rayon isn't as durable as the others.

Simplicity was the design goal in putting together this room, even though it took some ingenuity to accomplish it.

Natural fabrics are easier to clean than synthetics. Avoid stains by shopping for fabrics treated for soil resistance.

EASE UP YOUR ROOMS

Home should be a quiet place to put your feet up, relax, and renew. Here are some tips for easing up your rooms.

855 To dress your rooms for comfort, think about your weekend wardrobe. Classically casual, sturdy cottons, and washed linens wear well.

856 Avoid a "hands-off" room by introducing touchable texture. Soft wrinkles and mottled finishes invite visitors to relax and explore.

857 Shop for plain-lined, high-quality upholstery for style that lasts.

858 Like people, rooms get happier when they're bathed in sunlight. Blinds let in the light and pale, glossy paint bounces it around.

859 For less formality, fill your rooms with separates rather than suits of furniture.

860 Uncomplicate style with unadorned surfaces. Furniture and cabinetry without curves and crevices is easy to clean as well as easy to look at. Rich woods and earthy colors keep modern design from becoming too slick and cold.

861 Knock down walls that obstruct family togetherness.

BONUS SIMPLICITY

When you fill your home with simple things, life there just seems to slow down and take on a more graceful quality.

DECORATING
DISPLAYS

862 VARY HEIGHTS, SHAPES, STYLES

In this gathering of the old, the new, and the unusual, a veneered 1940s chest and a skyscraper of a chair make a lovely pair thanks to the clean, up-and-down lines they have in common—and the right-size accessory. Although the substantial glass vase might have made the small chest top-heavy, here it's an eye-appealing bridge between chest and chair.

PICTURE HANGING DO'S AND DON'TS

863 Do hang pictures at eye level. In a hallway, for example, the center of the artwork should be at eye level when standing; in a sitting area, put art at seated eye level.

864 Don't leave a gaping wall space between art and furniture. Pictures should be no more than a foot above furnishings so that you see the grouping as one unit.

865 Do fill in the wall space with a vase or other decorative object if you hang a picture high on a wall above a table. This links the table to the picture in a unified composition.

866 Don't ignore the space around the picture. For example, a few small pictures disappear on a large wall. Keep art in proportion to the wall.

867 Do create an eye-pleasing composition with several pictures or objects. Three items in a V-shape (for example, a picture over a sofa with a lamp on each side) lead the eye in a smooth, calming fashion. Or unify and organize a composition by framing different-size pictures in same-size frames. With a grouping of different-size frames, form straight vertical lines on the outer edges of the grouping.

868 Don't start hammering until you have a plan. First trace around the frame on a piece of paper, mark where the hook is, and cut out the form. Place the paper on the wall; when it's where you want it, nail away.

 KEEP ON PLAYING

The trick to artful displays and collages is to keep playing until they please your eye.

869 LIVING WITH THE THINGS YOU LOVE

If a personal look is what you're after, don't expect it to happen overnight. When you want an instant room, you end up with a showroom. It's better to build a scheme piece by piece as you find things you love. Let the room come to you.

870 CONSIDER ATTITUDE

For great displays, remember that what objects share is as important as how they differ. Look for similar attitudes (as in the hand-hewn quality of these pieces *left and below*) and color but vary heights and sizes for interest.

Fill up a given space for impact, but use a mix of shapes, textures, and sizes for interest.

BONUS MIX TEXTURES

Just as crackers add bite to soup, a mix of textures visually flavors a melting pot of styles. Link rough stuff (prickly cactus, a woolly blanket) with slick picks (black leather, icy glass) using shared colors and shapes to make opposites attractive.

GREAT MANTEL DISPLAYS

Magnetic mantels sometimes draw more knickknacks than adoring gazes. If your mantel looks lifeless, cluttered, or out of control, try some of these secrets for putting together artful displays.

871 **1.** Edit down your things so you're not displaying every collectible and knickknack at once.

872 **2.** Have a sense of humor! Mix serious collectibles with fun, unusual, or unexpected items.

873 **3.** Make a picture on the wall part of the display by hanging it just inches above the mantel. For a cohesive grouping, use tall objects that reach up to meet and even overlap your wall hanging.

874 **4.** Stagger and overlap objects rather than placing them in a boring row. Even within the small 8-inch depth of a mantel shelf, there's room to create different planes of space by pulling some objects forward and pushing others back.

875 **5.** Don't block the view of the main item by placing objects at dead center. Vary shapes and sizes of objects leading the eyes toward the focal point.

876 **6.** Use unequal numbers. Place more items on one side of the mantel than on the other. To give the grouping eye-pleasing balance and cohesiveness, place objects in loose triangular arrangements.

877 **7.** Give the eye a stopping point. For example, rest the last item in a display at an angle when all other pieces sit parallel to each other. Juxtaposing one item against the others creates a "period" at the end of the "sentence."

878 ROMANCE A WINDOW

Romance a window with this sheer covering that softens the view but won't interfere with special architecture or furniture. To create it, hide a standard tension rod inside 1-inch PVC pipe that has been shirred with fabric. Be sure to sand off any lettering on the pipe that will show through the fabric. Then stitch large wooden café rings to a hemmed panel of inexpensive, polyester sheer fabric and hang from the pipe to invite light to filter through with a dreamy, shimmering quality.

DESIGN IDEA
879 USE COPPER PIPE

Make curtain rods from copper pipe. For about $3 for an 8-foot length, it's a bargain that looks great. If you want, glue inexpensive brass-look finials (actually plastic, but who can tell from a distance) on the ends of the rods.

MONEY $ MATTERS
USE GAUZE

BONUS When the budget is tight, use gauze for a window treatment. Gauze is especially lovely in a room that has lots of natural light. It is inexpensive enough (usually $2 to $4 per yard) that you can afford to use plenty for a luxurious feeling.

BONUS Another hint is to use spray starch to give gauze great shape and fullness. You can highlight the gauze with gold spray paint.

880 COUNTRY CAFES

Ties sewn in the top edges of these curtains serve as easy hangers and add country style.

The curtains are simple to make. Just sew the hangers to the top edge of one rectangular piece of fabric; then stitch a second rectangle to the first. Turn inside out.

881 BAY WINDOW TREATMENT

Bay windows are tricky to decorate. The best way to cover those bumped-out panes is to treat them individually rather than as one block of windows. For privacy, great sun-blocking power, and to enhance the architectural appeal of your bays, choose miniblinds or pleated shades. Mount them inside the window molding for the cleanest looking, most energy-efficient treatment. A local window fabricator can create custom-colored shades or blinds in custom-made sizes. Or look for ready-made treatments at a discount store.

If you like fabric at the windows, you can top off your shades or blinds with a valance or swag. Mount the topper across the entire bank of windows in your bay to unify the panes and soften their look.

DESIGN IDEA
882 THE SIMPLICITY OF SLATS

Window treatments with slats have two practical attributes that make them especially well suited to bedrooms: privacy and light control. Shutters, horizontal blinds, and vertical blinds can all be easily adjusted to let in exactly the amount of natural light you wish. Plus, the adjustability of slatted treatments makes it possible for you to gain light without feeling as though you're on display—a definite advantage over their open-or-closed curtain counterparts.

Often mounted inside the window casing, slatted coverings are good candidates when the woodwork is too pretty to hide. They're also a good choice if you plan to place a piece of furniture under the window; unlike a long, fabric treatment, a fitted covering will stay out of the way.

Despite their sleek appearance shutters and blinds aren't solely for contemporary interiors. They're available in a variety of materials such as wood, aluminum, and vinyl, and in colors to coordinate with virtually any scheme. Some blinds can even be ordered with hardware-concealing cloth tapes in a wide range of colors and patterns.

Slat widths vary, too, from sleek ½-inch microblinds to shutters with 3-inch louvers. Some styles—wooden blinds with large slats, for example—are especially striking when used alone and add architectural interest to a plain space. Others work well in tandem with other treatments such as a valance or draperies.

In keeping with the airy, country spirit of this bedroom, white plantation shutters allow light to pour in through a wall of windows yet can be adjusted when the sunshine becomes too intense.

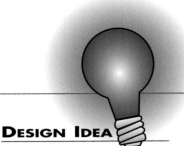

883 AN EASY-SEW SWAG

The breezy window treatment won't interfere with bathing in this countryside treetop-level bath where privacy isn't an issue. An easy-sew swag, made from a satin-stripe sheet, was stretched between two cup hooks and then knotted. To create the fluffy bottom edges, the fabric was looped up; raw ends were tucked into the corner knots.

BONUS FILTER LIGHT WITH LATTICE

If the view leaves something to be desired, try this striking inexpensive window treatment. Two 4x8 sheets of lattice (costing about $20 each at home supply stores) were cut to size, framed, sanded, spray painted, and set into the window frames (they lift out so the windows can be opened or closed). To make panels like these, first measure your window opening. Next, position that measurement on the panel, lining up the center of the measurement on the center of a wood strip or in the center of an opening. Then cut the panel using a table saw or circular saw. To build a frame for the lattice panel, sandwich the edges between a top and bottom wood strip; nail the strips to the panel. Paint or stain. To hold the panel in place in the window, attach hooks to the top of the window frame and hang the panel from the hooks.

MEASURE TO ORDER

With the wide variety of window dressings on the market today, measuring properly for new window treatments can be tricky. Here are some tips to ensure that your purchases measure up.

884 HARDWARE

Because drapery rods often extend beyond the width of the window and rings can alter the length of a curtain, drapery hardware needs to be included in your measurements.

Drapery rods can be mounted on the wall, on the window casing, inside the casing, or on the ceiling, depending on the treatment you choose.

A rod can also extend well beyond the window width for a more dramatic impact; the draperies "stack" beyond the sides of the window. To figure the stackback, divide the width of the glass by 3 and add 12 inches. This gives the total stacking area for a pair of draperies. Then to position the rod, divide the stackback figure in half and mark that distance from the outside edges of the glass. The distance between marks will be the length of rod you'll need.

885 DRAW DRAPERIES

To figure the finished width, measure the rod from bracket to bracket. Add 4 inches for an overlap at the center plus the depth of the returns on each end (omit the overlap for one-way draws).

To figure the length of draperies hung by hooks on conventional traverse or curtain rods, measure from the top of the installed rod. For decorative rods or café rods with rings, measure from the bottom of the rings. As a rule, curtains reach to the sill, apron, or floor, but fabric can also puddle gracefully on the floor.

886 CAFE CURTAINS

Measure the width of the rods between the finials. To determine the finished length of the top tier, measure from the lower part of the clip or ring on the upper rod to 3 to 6 inches below the clip or ring on the lower rod. (If you're using decorative rods or rings, measure only to the top of the lower rod.) For the lower tier, measure from the bottom of the ring on the lower rod to the desired finished length.

887 SHIRRED CURTAINS

Figure the finished length by measuring from 1 inch above the rod to the desired length. Measure 2 to 3 times the window width to allow for fullness.

Likewise for casements or French doors, measure the length from the top of the upper rod to the bottom of the lower rod. Measure the rod width inside the brackets and add $1\frac{1}{2}$ to 3 times to the width to allow for fullness.

888 BALLOON AND ROMAN SHADES

These two styles are commonly mounted on or above the casing. Measure the length from the top of the rod to the sill. The finished width should be even with (or $\frac{1}{2}$ inch wider than) the outside edges of the window casing.

889 DECORATIVE SCARF

For a decorative scarf—a single piece of fabric—measure the distance from the bottom of the drapery ring or the top of the decorative rod to the desired length of the scarf. Multiply that measurement by 2 and add 10 inches to each side if you want the fabric to puddle on the floor. Finally, measure the width of the area to be covered and add that figure to the length for the total yardage needed.

890 BLINDS

For inside-mounted miniblinds, a flat, 1-inch-deep surface is needed inside the casing to install brackets. Measure the distance between casings where the brackets are mounted to find the width. Then measure the length from inside the top casing to the sill.

For vertical blinds, measure the length from about 4 inches above the window (for hardware) to about 1 inch above the floor (for clearance). Measure width to the outside edges of the casing and add 2 to 4 inches to cover the side stackback.

SYSTEMS
HEATING

NEW AIR FILTERS

In the past, your choice of furnace and air-conditioning filters was limited. You could opt for either the 50-cent disposable filter or the $500 electronic variety.

Now, however, you can get a filter in the $10 to $30 range that captures 95 percent of the dust, dander, pollen, and other particles that loft through your house. Of these new air filters, there are two types to shop for—pleated and electrostatic.

891 Electrostatic filter
When air passes through the fabric of these filters it creates a small electrostatic charge. This charge acts like a magnet and traps small particles. Self-charging electrostatic fibers need no electricity to operate. Simply slide them in the slot where your regular filter fits. To clean, remove the filter and backwash it with a hose or shower. Cleaning is recommended about every 30 days. These filters generally last three to five years. Prices range from $30 to $50.

OUR ENVIRONMENT

ASBESTOS INSULATION WRAP

BONUS Check hot-water pipes and steam pipes that feed radiators in older houses. They may be insulated with a material containing asbestos. Look for a gray, corrugated, cardboard-like material or a chalky white material covering pipes. If the product is in good shape and has little likelihood of becoming damaged, just leave it alone.

BONUS If, however, the wrap is in an area where it could easily be bumped or damaged, you'll need to encapsulate (or wrap) the material. There are many commercial encapsulating products on the market such as fiberglass tape you dip in water and wrap around the pipe insulation. The tape hardens as it dries to form a barrier.

BONUS When wrapping insulation, you should always wear a respirator that has filters labeled "Approved for asbestos-laden dust." No other face mask will completely protect you.

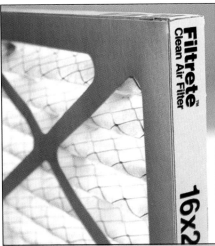

892 Pleated filters
Pleated filters are disposable, but they trap up to 95 percent of airborne particles. Their pleated contours and a fine mesh fabric expand the total surface area used for filtering and help trap particles as small as five microns (about $\frac{1}{100}$ the size of the head of a pin). Some pleated filters also carry an electrostatic charge. Pleated filters cost from $6 to $20 and usually last up to three months.

893 Plenty of benefits
Cutting back on indoor air particles brings relief for many allergy sufferers. Better air filtration will also reduce the amount of dusting you do in your home. Another benefit: your air-conditioning and heating equipment will stay cleaner and operate more efficiently.

MONEY $ MATTERS

CONSERVE ENERGY

Your home's size and insulation levels, locally available heating fuels, and the many efficiency levels of today's furnaces make it hard to tell when cutting costs on a replacement heating system is the right thing to do.

894 Generally, the higher the efficiency of the furnace or boiler, the higher the price. If you live in a house that is tough to insulate (such as a 1930s masonry veneer house) or if the climate is cold enough, the expense of a high-efficiency furnace will pay for itself quickly.

A furnace or boiler's efficiency is measured by an annual fuel utilization efficiency (AFUE) rating. Units with AFUEs in the 90 percent range are the most costly and you won't get your payback anytime soon. Cutting costs here may make sense unless you're living in an uninsulated Victorian in northern Minnesota.

895 Heating units above 90 percent efficiency are substantially higher priced than the next step down, which have an AFUE of around 85 percent. This is still an efficient heating system but look at the cost of fuel in your region to find the best option. In New England, for example, a 95 percent AFUE propane system would cost 25 percent more to run than a 91 percent AFUE oil system because fuel oil is cheaper there than propane.

896 Confused? Have your heating contractor figure out the "cost per million BTUs" for each available fuel. That way you're comparing apples to apples. It's an easy formula so if your heating contractor can't do it, find a new heating contractor.

897 Air conditioners are electricity guzzlers—pay special attention to their energy-efficiency ratings. Compare manufacturers' claims when shopping and compare cost and energy efficiency against payback. Payback for a more efficient air conditioner is much quicker than for a high-efficiency furnace. Summer electrical rates keep rising making high-efficiency air-conditioning a good short- or long term-investment.

OUR ENVIRONMENT

SAVE OUR RESOURCES

A few simple tips can help you keep expenses down and save energy.

BONUS Turn down the thermostat on your water heater to 120 degrees to save energy and help prevent scalding.

BONUS Change the filter on your air conditioner often. A dirty filter substantially cuts energy efficiency.

BONUS To increase air flow, keep the area in front of air-circulation registers clear of furniture and draperies.

HOME HEATING CHECKLIST

Don't wait til midwinter to check your home's heating system. Tackle the do-it-yourself maintenance early to keep your family warm and cozy.

898 Install a new furnace filter so that clean, warm air can circulate freely. A throwaway filter catches up to 10 percent of the dirt particles in the air and needs to be replaced every three months during the heating season. A semipermanent media (treated paper or plastic fiber) filter collects 35 percent of the particles and should be replaced or cleaned about every two months. Permanent electrostatic filters trap 90 percent of the dust and require little maintenance.

899 Inspect the ducts while the filter is off and sweep out any dirt or dust.

Vacuum the summer's dust and dirt from grilles and registers.

900 Clean the furnace humidifier and check its operation. A properly-working humidifier puts moisture in the warm air that makes you feel warmer and keeps furniture from drying out.

901 Check all the duct and flue connections that you can see to make sure they're not leaking. To keep heated air from cooling off on its trip from the furnace, wrap the hot-air ducts with special insulating blankets.

902 Turn on the furnace burner and furnace fan to see if they run smoothly and quietly.

903 Look through the furnace access door and check the chimney for soot accumulation. If you see a thick buildup on the chimney walls, call a chimney sweep.

904 Tightly close the furnace access door after your inspection.

If you uncover any problems or you suspect your furnace is malfunctioning, call a heating contractor for a professional inspection.

SAVE MONEY: USE LESS FUEL

905 Use a programmable thermostat to control indoor temperature fluctuations to suit your lifestyle.

906 To block winter winds and cut heating costs, plant evergreens on the north and west sides of your home or between the house and the coldest winds.

• Upgrade from a 60-percent-efficient furnace to an 80-percent-efficient one to reduce heating costs by a third. Upgrade to a 90-percent-efficient unit to reduce costs by about half.

907 Replacing a heating system is not a small investment. Many utilities help customers obtain funding for their projects as long as high-efficiency equipment is installed. In many cases, payments for these loans can be included in monthly utility bills.

TROUBLESHOOTING A FORCED-AIR SYSTEM

Tucked into utility rooms, inside walls, and under floors, the machines that heat and cool our homes are all too easy to forget. They'll pop back into mind, however, when something goes awry.

With forced-air heating and cooling systems, problems can be easy to fix or can require professional help. Solving the problem can be as simple as raising the thermostat or flushing out debris that blocks a coil. Check out the chart below for the causes of and solutions for some common problems. It's wise to try out all the options before calling a professional.

Problem	Causes	Solutions
908 **No heat**	No fuel. Thermostat set too low. Circuit breaker or furnace switch open; fuse blown. Pilot out. Oil-burner motor overheated.	Raise thermostat 5 degrees. Check for electrical problem; then throw breaker, replace fuse, or reset furnace switch. If it goes out again, call a professional. Relight gas pilot. Add oil to oil-burner motor. Restart motor.
909 **No cool air**	Blower runs: lack of refrigerant, clogged filter, or debris blocking outdoor condenser. System silent: electrical fault.	Recharging with refrigerant requires service. Change dirty filter; hose out debris from condensing unit. Check for electrical overload, reset the breaker, or change fuse. If electrical problem recurs, call for service.
910 **System cycles on and off too often**	Clogged filter, malfunctioning blower, or faulty thermostat. Causes are the same for heating and cooling.	Check and change filter. Examine blower motor for slow response and blower fan for scraping, sticking, or off-center rotation. Clean thermostat contacts; call for service if that fails to work.
911 **Uneven distribution of heating, cooling**	Airflow out of balance.	Try to balance system by adjusting register dampers. If this doesn't work, have professional rebalance ducts.
912 **Excessive furnace noise**	Squealing: fan belt slippage, dry bearings or motor. Rumbling: pilot needs adjusting. Rattling: blower speed set too fast.	Tighten fan belt. Oil bearings. Add oil to motor cups for oil burner. Adjust pilot flame until it's mostly blue with a yellow tip. Call for service to clean burners. Lower fan speed if blower is variable.
913 **Frequent heat pump defrost cycles**	Ice is blocking outdoor coil.	Ice may be collecting on leaves, seeds, and other matter jammed into coils. Clean by hosing out the debris. If the coils are clear and the heat pump continues to defrost frequently, the unit might have a faulty reversing valve. Call a professional to check the valve.

BEFORE YOU FIRE UP, CHECK THE FIREPLACE

Love your fireplace? You're in good company. But before you light that first fire of the season, heed the following advice.

914 First have your fireplace system thoroughly inspected. A professional chimney sweep or house inspector can uncover potential house-fire hazards. Bird nests between the metal lining and wooden frame of factory-built fireplace systems are common culprits as are less-visible cracked or broken linings in masonry fireplaces.

915 Many chimneys, especially those made before the 1930s, need relining. (Some 19th-century homes may have no lining at all.) The job costs about $2,000. Have your inspector or chimney sweep check to see that a brick barrier (called a wythe) separates the flues when two fireplaces or a furnace and a fireplace share a common chimney. This barrier acts as a firewall and will help to contain a serious chimney fire.

916 Install a chimney rain cap. It keeps out varmints, as well as rainwater. That's important because water mixed with acidic fire residues can destroy the mortar in fireplace brickwork.

917 If your fireplace doesn't seem to "draw," it probably isn't getting enough outside air or your chimney isn't positioned to get a cross-wind at the top of the flue (that's how a fire-encouraging "draft" is created). To remedy the problem, crack a window somewhere in the room before starting a fire.

918 When smoke "backs up" as you're starting a fire, your flue probably isn't properly warmed up, allowing cold chimney air to rush down into the fireplace. Remedy: 10 to 15 minutes before you light a fire, open the damper to let in more air.

919 When burning wood, choose the hardwoods like oak, hickory, locust, or elm. These woods leave behind limited amounts of sticky, flammable creosote. Don't burn soft, sappy woods such as cottonwood, pine, or apple.

COOLING/VENTILATION

920 NATURALLY COOL

Putting your daily routine and the design of your house in tune with nature can reduce cooling costs and summer discomfort. The drawing *below* shows how to tune into Mother Nature's cooling methods.

1. Chimney exhausts hot air.
2. Gable vent allows attic heat to escape.
3. Deciduous trees shade south side of house in summer.
4. Overhangs protect windows on south side.
5. Screened porch shields interior of house from sun.
6. Shrubs shade air conditioner.
7. When closed, operable shutters block heat.

8. North window opened a little draws fresh air into house.
9. Recessed entry protects living areas from wind and sun.
10. Shrubs between walkway and windows absorb heat reflected from sidewalk.
11. Garage eliminates need for windows on northeast side.
12. Light-colored roof reflects heat.

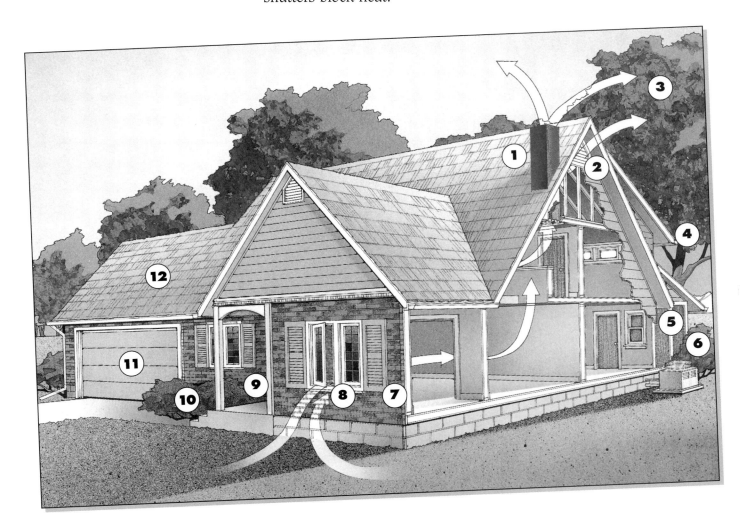

CROSS VENTILATION

Even when air is at a higher temperature than you consider ideal, it will feel cooler as it moves across your skin than when it is stagnant. This is because the moisture in your skin evaporates as air crosses it. As the moisture evaporates it absorbs heat, leaving your skin cooler.

You can get the same effect by creating air movement through your house. Here are some guidelines.

921 Open windows across from each other. Compared to opening windows on only one side of the house, opening opposite windows is three times more effective in creating a cross breeze.

922 When possible, open a window low on the cool side of the house and high on the hot side. This creates a cooling air current. In the early morning, for instance, open a window low on the west side and high on the east side. In the afternoon, reverse the process.

923 Keep the opening on the cooler side of the house fairly small; as an air current passes through a small opening it picks up velocity, creating more of a breeze.

924 Make sure trees and shrubs are trimmed so they do not block ventilation. Ideally the air current should be able to go below the branches of shade trees and above shrubs.

MONEY $ MATTERS
SAVE COOLING DOLLARS

Even if your air-conditioning system is new, small expenditures can reduce the call for cooling.

925 Install a programmable thermostat that can be preset to lower the temperature before you return home and raise it after you've left.

926 Check the filter each month during the cooling season. Replace when it's clogged with dust and dirt.

927 Keep a regular maintenance schedule; it's best to hire a professional to check your air-conditioning system each spring.

Keep your energy costs down—develop good habits.

928 Operate appliances (washers, dryers, ovens) during the coolest hours of the morning or evening.

929 Pull draperies and shades shut over windows and doors that face the sun.

930 Use an exhaust fan to remove excess heat and humidity from the kitchen and bathrooms.

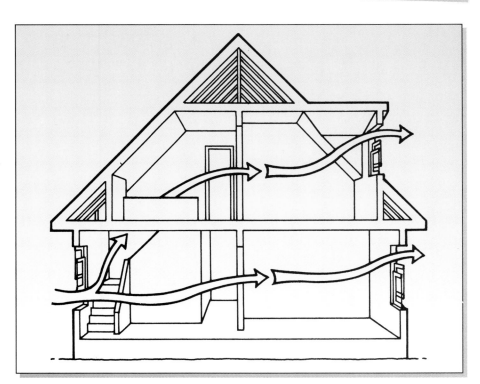

BONUS Open windows to capture night-time breezes and rid your house of summer heat. Channeling prevailing breezes through an arrangement of low-venting windows and high-venting windows *(above)* is the cheapest summer cooling strategy available.

Low and high vents work even better in attics, where temperatures are higher and interior space is more open for freer circulation. Install about 1 square foot of vent opening per 300 square feet of attic floor area.

KEEP COOL WITH A WHOLE-HOUSE FAN

Six to eight degrees of cooling and a slight breeze can make a world of difference in summer comfort. Whole-house fans provide soothing lower temperatures while consuming far less electricity than an average air conditioner

931 House fans are most useful when outdoor temperatures range from the mid-70s to the mid-80s. To gauge your cooling needs calculate the cubic feet of air moved per minute (CFM). Multiply the square footage of your home by three to get the CFM. A house of 1,500 square feet, for example, needs a fan that delivers 4,500 CFM. In warm climates or Sunbelt states, multiply your square footage by four.

932 You'll also need adequate attic vents to expel the air. To calculate the required vent space, divide your CFM by 750. This gives you the number of square feet of attic space needed (double that size if vents are screened or louvered).

933 Most average do-it-yourselfers can install a whole-house fan but hire an electrician for the wiring. When shopping, look for belt-driven motors, ball-bearing construction, and rubber motor mounts for years of quiet, trouble-free service.

USE CEILING FANS

A ceiling fan saves energy in summer and winter. Its cooling breeze in summer lets you run the air conditioner less. Air that is in motion feels 4 degrees cooler than stagnant air. This means with a proper-size fan you can increase the thermostat setting 4 degrees without sacrificing comfort. Fans use much less energy than air conditioners so you'll see a significant reduction in overall energy costs.

BONUS Reverse blades in winter to circulate heated air trapped near the ceiling. During winter months, set your fan at the slowest speed. This setting will gently push the warm air down from the ceiling without whipping up an unwelcome breeze.

BONUS A fan with a 36- or 38-inch blade span is adequate for a room measuring 10x10 feet or less; a room up to 15x20 feet needs a 48-, 52-, or 54-inch-diameter fan.

BONUS Measurements: For physical safety and psychological comfort, install your fan at least 7 feet above the floor. Most fans extend between 12 and 24 inches from the ceiling, so your selection will probably be influenced by the height of your ceilings.

OUR ENVIRONMENT

934 # GET THE LEAD OUT OF YOUR WATER

Be wary of scam artists touting free tests and trying to sell you treatment systems you don't need. The wisest course of action is to use a lab certified by your state or the Environmental Protection Agency (EPA). A typical test costs $15 to $25. EPA guidelines recommend taking steps to purify your water if it tests for lead above 20 parts per billion.

TROUBLESHOOTING WATER HEATERS

Problem	Solution
Water won't heat (electric)	**935** Check the fuse box or circuit breaker for a blown fuse or tripped switch; reactivate. If the heater continues to blow fuses or circuits often, call in a pro.
Water won't heat (gas)	**936** Pilot light isn't burning; relight it. Unclog burner ports as explained below. Make sure the gas connection shutoff valve is fully open. Check temperature control for proper setting.
Water is too hot	**937** Check the thermostat setting; turn back setting, if necessary. The thermostat may be malfunctioning or not functioning at all. If you suspect this, call a professional.
Water tank is leaking	**938** Turn off the heater's water and gas or electrical supplies and drain the tank. It'll probably have to be replaced.
Water supply pipes leak	**939** Tighten the pipe fittings. If this doesn't work, turn off the water and replace fittings. If the water is condensing on the water supply pipe, wrap the pipe with standard pipe insulation.
Clogged gas burner ports	**940** Remove the debris with a needle or the end of a paper clip. Do not use a wooden toothpick or peg; either can break off in the portholes.
Gas flame burns yellow	**941** The burner may not be getting enough primary air. Check the pilot light; the flame should be about ½ inch long. Call in a pro for any necessary adjustments. The burner of a gas water heater should be serviced professionally every 24 months or so.
Heater smells of gas	**942** Immediately turn off the gas at the main supply valve. Open the windows and let the gas out. Turn on the gas at the main valve and coat the pipe connections with soapy water. If bubbles appear, the connection is leaking. Do not relight until the gas leak has been repaired.

CONSERVING WATER

Water covers three-fourths of our planet but less than 1 percent of it is available for human use. As pressures from population growth and pollution continue to grow, the cost of finding and purifying our water is increasing.

Simple home conservation measures can easily cut your water use in half and save your family hundreds of dollars a year in water bills. Here's how.

943 In the bathroom

More than 75 percent of our water is used in the bathroom. Toilets are the worst water guzzlers. Older toilets use 5 to 6 gallons per flush. Models built since the 1970s use about 3.5 gallons. The old trick of putting a brick in the tank, however, is not recommended. Submerged bricks disintegrate and this grit can jam your toilet's working parts. Any tampering with the water level can lead to unsanitary conditions and subject your home to sewer odors.

944 Low-flow technology

The best water saver for the bathroom is a low-flow toilet that uses only 1.5 to 1.6 gallons. It costs about the same as a regular toilet but it eventually pays for itself by reducing water bills. Retrofitting existing toilets with new flappers—the rubber valves that seal the tank—also helps reduce water use.

945 Showers

The biggest consumer of hot water in your home is the shower. Older shower heads deliver up to 8 gallons per minute. Shop for a newer shower head that puts out 3 gallons or less per minute, 14,000 gallons per year, and $80 in water heating costs. Prices range from $10 to $50. Water-saving shower heads are preferable to flow restrictors that insert between the shower head and the shower arm. Restrictors may result in a weaker spray.

946 At the sink

Don't leave water running while you brush your teeth, shave, or wash your face. Fill the sink rather than use a constant stream. This simple procedure can save your family as much as 2,000 gallons a year.

947 Clothes washers

Front-load washers use 33 percent less water than top-load washers. For the average family of four, this adds up to a savings of 3,000 gallons a year. Be mindful of the water-level settings you use on the washer you have now. Don't wash a medium load on a higher setting—a mistake people frequently make.

948 Dishwashing

Washing dishes by hand takes about 16 gallons of water. The same dishes can be cleaned in a dishwasher with 7 to 10 gallons. Reduce your savings by prerinsing or washing less than full loads.

949 Faucet aerators

A faucet aerator can cut water use in half, and save up to 100 gallons a year per faucet. Aerators slow a conventional faucet's flow down to about 2 gallons per minute. Aerators for kitchen and bath faucets can be found in most hardware stores. They cost between $2 and $10 and simply screw onto your faucet nozzle.

950 Check for leaks

On your next trip away from home, check for leaks in your water system. Write down the numbers on your water meter when you leave, and check the meter again upon returning. If it has moved at all, you have a leak.

Your first suspect should be the toilet. Add a few drops of a nonstaining dye to water in the tank. If the color shows up in the bowl or if it's gone after a few hours, you have a leak. Check the flush-ball or flapper and replace if necessary. A sheet of paper left under a faucet overnight will indicate a leak there. Also check water supply lines and fittings inside your cabinets for signs of dampness. If you can't find the leak, call a plumber. Undetected leaks can cause structural damage and attract termites and carpenter ants.

951 Outdoor water use

Water your lawn and garden early in the morning. Watering during the day loses water to evaporation and watering at night may lead to fungus or mildew problems. For efficient and hassle-free watering, install trickle irrigation and timed sprinklers. Ground covers and other drought-tolerant landscaping methods greatly reduce summer water demand.

BONUS STOP TOILET LEAKS

The flush ball at the bottom of your toilet water tank may be leaking a small but steady stream of water—sometimes thousands of gallons a year. To stop these expensive leaks all you need to do is replace the flush ball with a flapper. These flexible rubber devices open and close the valve at the bottom of the tank like a flush ball but they seal watertight. A flapper costs $2 to $3 and can be installed (in most cases) without tools. If you already have a flapper or a similar device in your tank, check it at least once a year to make sure it remains flexible.

COPING WITH PRESSURE PROBLEMS

Water pressure is one of those things you can have too much or too little of. Too little pressure results in trickles rather than streams of water, with obvious results. Too much (a much rarer problem) wrecks faucets and weakens connections in your system.

If you have too little pressure and if your water source is a well with an electric pump, the pressure regulator at the pump may be set too low. Also check for a loose pump belt. In the winter low pressure can be caused by a frozen pipe or pressure switch.

If none of the obvious checks produces results, break a connection in the water system. If you find lime deposits inside the pipe, you may have to finance a new plumbing job. Under no circumstances should you try to flush a limed system with chemicals. You can have sediment flushed from the pipes, though, which may restore much of the pressure. This is a job for a professional plumber; don't attempt to do it yourself.

If liming is a problem in your area, the cheapest and easiest way to correct it is to install a water softener on cold as well as hot lines.

Before calling in a plumber, call water department officials and ask them to check the water main leading into your home. It could be faulty.

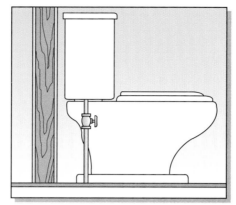

952 Make sure all supply valves are open. Also turn off water at the main and check valve parts for damage, corrosion, or liming.

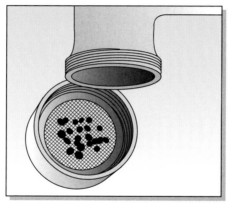

953 Unscrew aerators on faucet spouts to clean out any debris. If the wire strainer is badly corroded, replace it.

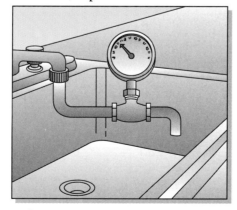

954 An inexpensive pressure gauge is a fast, easy way to check water pressure. It should register 50 to 60 pounds per square inch.

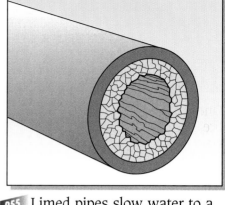

955 Limed pipes slow water to a trickle. If flushing the system doesn't help, you'll have to have your house re-plumbed.

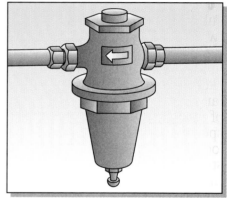

956 To decrease pressure, buy a pressure-reducing valve. The farther open the valve, the less pressure you should have.

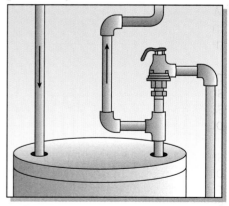

957 If your water heater doesn't have a relief valve, install one. Without one, hot water pressure could reach dangerous levels.

REPAIRING FAUCETS IN YOUR HOUSE

One of the most common breakdowns in a household water supply is a faulty diverter in the faucet. Whether the spout needs to be replaced or simply adjusted, the repair is a relatively minor one once you understand how the mechanism works.

Tub/Shower Diverters

Tub/shower diverters fall into two classifications. One group, typified by the stem-type valve in the upper portion of the sketch *right,* is housed in the faucet body and directs the flow of water from there. Tub diverter spouts, on the other hand, are located farther out on the main spout and act independently of the faucet.

The sketches show how each type works. In the closed position the diverter valve (located on the stem) blocks off water flow to the shower head. When it's fully opened, it diverts incoming water to the shower head.

Diverter mechanisms vary by manufacturer, but whatever the style they all operate much the same way and serve the same purpose.

With the type of tub diverter spout illustrated *right,* lifting up on its knob while the water is running seals off the inlet to the spout and forces the water up to and out of the shower head. Continued water pressure maintains the seal. When the water is shut off, the knob will drop back into its usual position.

958 When a tub diverter spout wears out or the lift rod attached to the knob breaks off from the plate it's attached to, you must replace the entire spout.

To remove the spout, insert a hammer handle into the opening. Use it to rotate the spout counterclockwise until it separates from the nipple. To ensure a tight seal, apply pipe compound around the nipple then install the new spout.

959 If a stem-type valve begins to leak or no longer diverts water properly, shut off water to the faucet (being sure to drain the lines), and remove the nut holding the stem in place. Withdraw the stem and inspect the packing washer (if your diverter has one) to see whether there are any worn-out parts that need to be replaced.

Sink Diverters

960 If nothing happens when you press the lever on your kitchen sink spray, you might have a worn-out diverter. First check to see that the hose isn't kinked, restricting the flow of water.

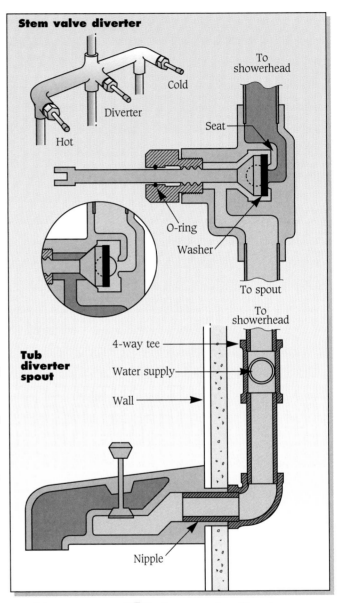

Stem valve diverter

To showerhead

Cold

Diverter

Hot

Seat

O-ring

Washer

To spout

Tub diverter spout

To showerhead

4-way tee

Water supply

Wall

Nipple

961 To inspect the diverter, disassemble the faucet body under the spout or in the spout itself. Replace faulty parts or the diverter itself, if necessary.

962 If the faucet parts seem to be in good repair, the problem might be that mineral deposits are restricting the flow of water through the spray. Clean the teeth of the spray disk with a straight pin and tighten all connections.

PROJECT PRIMER

BONUS REPLACING A FAUCET

Replacing a faucet is a simple task that requires only a beginner's know-how. Several specialized tools make the job easier: a basin wrench, pipe wrenches, a tubing cutter for copper pipe and riser tubing (pipes that carry water from the shutoff valve to the sink), pipe joint compound, a spiral tubing bender to shape the risers, screwdrivers, a small hacksaw, adjustable wrenches, a faucet seat wrench, groove-joint pliers, and thread pipe.

To remove an old faucet, first turn off the water supply valves and lay an old towel beneath the sink to catch water trapped in the risers. Unfasten the coupling nut at the top of each riser to disconnect it from the faucet shank. Then undo the mounting or jamb nuts on the shanks that secure the faucet to the deck of the sink. Lift the old faucet out and scrape putty from the sink where the old faucet sat. Finally undo the bottom nuts on the risers so you can remove them from the shutoff valves.

To install the new faucet, carefully follow the directions that came with the model. Most faucets are secured with jamb nuts on the shanks or on bolts that protrude from the base. Slip the bottom plate or gasket into place and drop the faucet into place. Then fasten it from below, making sure the faucet base is parallel to the edge of the deck before tightening the nuts.

Connect the faucet to the water supply using risers of flexible metal tubing that connect with compression fittings. To seat the risers tightly their length should be slightly longer than the distance from the valve to the water intakes on the faucet. After coating the ends with plumber's putty, insert the bottom ends of the risers into the shutoff valves and the top ends into the faucet shanks and tighten the coupling nuts onto the shanks.

To test your connections, slowly open the shutoff valves and turn on the faucet.

PLUMBING PRECAUTIONS FOR WINTER VACATIONS

In climates where temperatures fall below 32° Fahrenheit, exposed pipes containing water will freeze and possibly burst. In times past, homeowners who were vacating for a month or two or even the entire winter, simply turned down the thermostat but left enough heat to keep pipes from freezing. Today, however, energy costs make that an expensive proposition. Fortunately, you can shut down your entire plumbing system and let the furnace remain on at a very low setting while you're away.

To determine whether it's likely that your pipes will freeze in your absence during winter months, check to see if any of these problem conditions apply to your plumbing:

963 The water supply line is not installed below the frost line.

964 Supply lines are installed in an unheated crawl space, not in a basement.

965 Piping is installed in outside walls in northern climates.

966 Outdoor faucets for hose connections are not connected to interior plumbing via a freeze-proof hydrant.

Even when none of these conditions exists, you should follow certain procedures before leaving your house unattended during cold months. The following five procedures will help keep your plumbing protected:

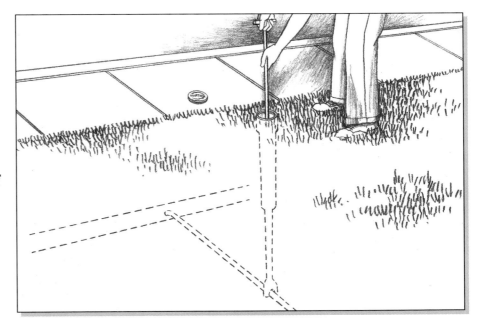

967 Call the water department and ask to have your service turned off at the valve outside your home *(see illustration, right)*. The department may want to remove the meter, too. If not, you can go ahead and close the valve on its supply side.

968 Now start at the top of your home's supply system and open every faucet to ensure that all the water is drained out *(see, illustration, center)*. Shut off power to the water heater and drain it. This saves on fuel bills and also extends the life of the heater, since it removes the sediment in the bottom of the tank that comes from particles settling in the water. (For maintenance, drain a few inches of water from the tank every six months.) Don't forget that the washing machine and dishwasher also need to be drained.

969 At the system's bottom, look for stop-waste valves near the water meter and elsewhere. Open the drain cock in each of these *(see illustration, center)*.

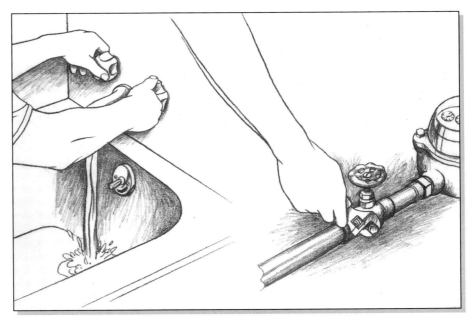

970 For pipes that are known problems, insulative jacketing or electrical heat tape will help. Cut jacketing to fit the length of the pipe and secure with plastic tape. Wrap heat tape around pipes and plug into an outlet. A thermostat turns the tape on and off as needed.

971 To keep fixture drain traps from freezing, add antifreeze mixed with water according to can directions. For a toilet, pour a gallon of antifreeze solution into the bowl to start the flushing action *(see illustration, right)*. Some solution remains in the trap. If your home has a main house trap, fill it with undiluted antifreeze *(see illustration, right)*.

PREVENTING PIPE FREEZE-UPS

You'll save yourself a lot of winter grief if you plan plumbing remodelings with a little thought to water pipe placement. The safest location is in an interior wall. If winter has already arrived and your plumbing is in a vulnerable location (such as an uninsulated exterior wall) you may have problems. Some of the steps below may get you through the cold season without water pipe leaks.

972 **1.** Electric heat tape, *top right*, contains a thermostat that maintains a constant temperature, usually about 70 degrees. Wrap the tape around the pipe and plug one end into an outlet. The tape draws only modest amounts of current. You can also hang a 100-watt trouble light (the kind used to work on automobiles) and direct it toward the pipe. Of course these solutions won't work during power outages when your home most needs protection against the cold.

973 **2.** Pipe jacketing and ordinary insulation, *center right,* work equally well. Cut pipe jacketing with a knife and secure with plastic electrical tape. Cut ordinary insulation in strips and tape it around the pipe. Be sure to insulate all joints and connections.

For an extremely cold wall or floor you may be better off packing the entire cavity with insulation. Insulating hot-water runs, especially any that pass through unheated spaces, is an easy way to conserve water-heating energy.

974 **3.** If a pipe starts to freeze before you take any preventive steps, crack open the faucet at the end of the lines you're concerned about and let water trickle through the pipes. (Running water won't freeze.) If there's a cabinet underneath, open its doors and let room heat warm the pipes, *(see illustration opposite, bottom)*. You can also hang a trouble light in the cabinet to warm the space around the pipes.

975 **If Your Pipes Freeze**
Thawing frozen pipes is a complicated job best left to an expert. Turn off the main water supply to your home even before you call for help. After the pipes thaw, you don't want water to leak out of the rupture.

If you decide to thaw out pipes yourself, use electric heat tape or a trouble light to slowly raise the temperature of the pipe. This will take time. Do not use a propane torch. It can create so much heat that the water in the pipes turns to steam causing an explosion. The open flame of the torch is dangerous; it can ignite nearby surfaces.

OUR ENVIRONMENT

BONUS # SWITCH TO COMPACT FLUORESCENT BULBS

Lighting accounts for 20 percent of the electricity used. Cut down energy use by keeping a log of which lights in the house get the most use and replace them with compact fluorescent bulbs that save energy.

• A 75-watt incandescent can be replaced by an 18-watt compact fluorescent.

• Incandescent lights throw out 17 to 22 lumens per watt of electricity compared with compact fluorescent bulbs which produce 65 to 100 lumens per watt.

• Only about 10 percent of the electricity consumed by an incandescent is turned into visible light. Most of the rest is turned into heat.

• Not only will compact fluorescent bulbs save energy, they last 7 times longer.

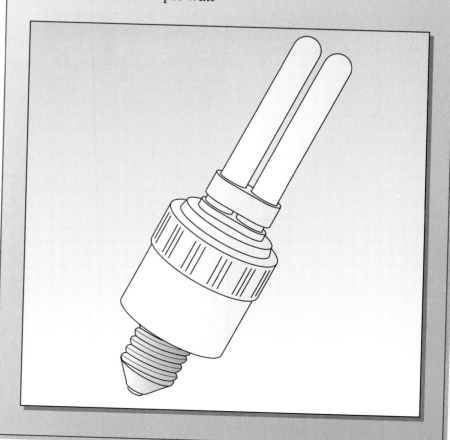

INSULATING OUTLETS

Here's a solution for one of the biggest energy wasters in your home—electrical outlets. Insulating foam gaskets cost just pennies and take less than a minute to install.

Regular fiberglass batt insulation leaves gaps around electrical boxes and wires. These gaps form conduits for cold outside air to shoot straight into your home.

976 To find out if your home needs foam gaskets on the outlets, wait for a cold, windy night; then, hold a candle or incense smoke near an outlet. Cold air infiltrating your home will cause the flame to bob and weave or the smoke from the incense to scatter or furl. If you've conscientiously weather-stripped your windows and doors your electrical outlets are now probably the weakest link in the thermal envelop of your home.

977 To install, simply remove the outlet cover plate with a screwdriver, press the gasket in place, and replace the cover plate. Most gaskets come in packages of five or 10.

PROJECT PRIMER

978 INSTALL A LIGHT FIXTURE

Replacing a light fixture sounds intimidating but once you remember to turn off the power to the circuit before you begin the project; analyze the existing wiring in the electrical box that supports a switch, outlet, or light fixture; and stock up on a few necessary tools, you can handle this job yourself.

There are a number of common fixture hookups. If there are only two wires in the electrical box—a black wire and a white wire—they lead directly from the switch or power supply. Simply use a twist connector to fasten the leads from your new fixture to the matching wires. The simplest fixture to install is one that mounts directly on the box and is connected to switch wires. One example of this is the white ceramic light socket, with or without a pull-chain switch, commonly used in basements, closets, and hallways.

If there are four wires in the box, two carry the incoming power and the other two form a loop that feed electrical current through the switch and back. The white incoming power wire connects to the white fixture. The black incoming power wire connects to the black wire that leads to the switch. The other wire leading to the switch (which you should also mark as "black" for future reference)

connects to the black fixture wire to complete the circuit.

If the wiring is more complex, make a diagram and label the wires before you undo the original connections. More complicated hookups—such as multiple-bulb fixtures, light-plus-receptacle fixtures, and light kits for ceiling fans—may require additional study.

Whatever fixture you're replacing, you'll find the work will go more smoothly with some basic tools: multipurpose tool to strip insulation, cut wire, and crimp wire connectors; a 120/140-volt voltage tester; and a continuity tester. A voltage tester lights up when power runs through it and is used to identify hot devices and wires with the circuit power off and on. A continuity tester is used only with the circuit power off and the fixture or component disconnected. The tester will light up if the device is good.

To run cable through finished walls and ceilings, use a flexible steel fish tape. You also will need twist connectors in assorted sizes, electrician's tape, a utility knife, Allen wrenches, and screwdrivers and pliers with handles *specifically* insulated for electrical work. Many tools have insulated grips that are for comfort only—they won't protect you from current.

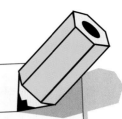

HIRING A PRO

Wiring is one of the most important parts of remodeling. Some remodeling contractors tell you they'll do the wiring themselves. If the contractor is a licensed electrician, that's fine.

979 If not, spend the additional money to hire a licensed electrician who can wire your house to comply with the strict rules of the National Electrical Code (NEC).

Most cities and towns require an inspection of new wiring to point out where mistakes were made and where upgrades are required. Here's where the extra dollars spent to hire a licensed electrician can spare you big headaches.

980 Don't dismiss this stage by thinking it's just another bureaucratic hassle—the inspection is for your own safety. Think of the inspector as a partner who's looking for shortcuts that can eventually turn into short circuits.

981 For example, one shortcut involves leaving exposed wires on walls or ceilings. "Exposed" in this case doesn't mean bare wire; a wire is considered exposed even if the jacketed cable is nailed along the wall. Wire should be placed either behind the wall surface or in conduit. If you see an exposed wire running anywhere, ask the electrical inspector if it's safe.

982 When remodeling your kitchen, don't be surprised if your local electrical code requires more circuits than the house originally had. With a microwave oven, refrigerator, dishwasher, and disposal, you'll need a minimum of seven circuits.

A shoddy contractor may put all the kitchen outlets on the same circuit but the NEC calls for two separate circuits for all wall outlets and separate circuits ("dedicated outlets") for major appliances. With dedicated outlets appliances can't overtax a circuit and trip the circuit breaker. Plus, if a kitchen outlet circuit trips the breaker the refrigerator will stay cold.

983 Here's another hint for wiring the kitchen: You need two circuits just for outlets so have the electrician wire every other outlet to one of the circuits. Then wire the remaining outlets to the second circuit. This way, if you run your toaster next to your blender, they won't be on the same circuit even though the outlets are next to each other.

984 If you are doing an extensive remodeling involving tearing walls down to bare studs, don't let a few extra dollars stand in the way of an opportunity to upgrade wiring. To do it later will cost a lot more and create a second mess.

985 If your house was built before 1945, you probably have 60-amp service with cloth-insulated wires separated by a foot of space (knob-and-tube wiring). When you upgrade you'll want 100-amp service assuming your major appliances are gas. And you'll probably find the electrical code requires installing a few more convenience outlets around bathroom sinks.

OUR ENVIRONMENT
CONSERVE ENERGY

BONUS Consider a motion-detector switch for lights that get left on accidentally. These devices cost about $10 to $15 and automatically turn off lights when a person leaves a room or hallway.

BONUS Use one high-wattage bulb rather than several low-wattage bulbs. A single 100-watt bulb uses the same energy as four 25-watt bulbs but produces more light.

SAFE OUTDOOR OUTLETS

Yard work is easier with power tools but play it safe: Install a ground fault circuit interrupter (GFCI) wherever you need an outdoor electrical outlet.

986 Wired into both of the conductors in a circuit, GFCI continuously compares current levels flowing through the hot and neutral sides. If the GFCI senses a difference of just 1/200 of an amp, it shuts off the electricity within 1/50 of a second. The GFCI deters an accident or tool malfunction from directing current through you on its way to the ground. That can happen, for example, if your hedge clippers have frayed wires inside. With a GFCI you may still get a shock but it won't be fatal.

987 If you've done electrical work before, you can install a GFCI. GFCIs are available at most home centers and hardware stores for about $20. Shop for a size that will fit your old receptacle's junction box. If you're installing a new outlet, any size will do.

988 Before removing the receptacle on your outdoor outlet, throw the master switch at the control panel and use a tester lamp to make sure the outdoor circuit is dead. Install the GFCI, *above center,* as you would a conventional receptacle, following the manufacturer's directions. When done, press the GFCI's test button to make sure you've wired it correctly.

TROUBLESHOOTING DOORBELLS AND CHIMES

Running down a problem in your doorbell (or chime) system is mainly a process of elimination.

989 If the bell works sporadically, check out the button first. Unscrew it from the wall and hold a screwdriver across the two contact points. If the bell doesn't ring, clean the contact points with emery cloth and make sure the contacts touch when the button is pushed.

990 Assuming the button works, check the bell and transformer for loose connections. If they're tight, hold a screwdriver across the transformer's bell-wire connections. If you don't get a weak spark, replace the transformer. If you do see even the faintest spark, the transformer is fine and your search narrows down to the bell itself or to the wiring. The easiest way to check the bell is to disconnect it, clean it thoroughly, rub the contacts with emery cloth, then hook it up directly to the bell-wire connections at the transformer. If you don't get a ring, the bell is shot; if you do, you'll need to replace the wire—a tedious, last resort.

991 REPLACING RECEPTACLES

If a receptacle goes bad and you're elected to replace it, all you need to do is wire the new outlet exactly as the old one. Note: In newer homes and some older ones, there's often a (third) ground wire that connects to the receptacle. This is an equipment ground wire.

Before you start, remember to turn off the power at the main disconnect or circuit breaker. Then remove the faceplate.

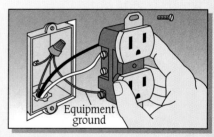

Equipment ground

Remove the screws fastening the receptacle to the box at top and bottom, and pull the receptacle from the box.

Before you disconnect anything, make a quick sketch

to help you remember where each wire goes. Then remove the wires.

Hook up the new receptacle using your sketch if needed. Test your handiwork by restoring power to the receptacle.

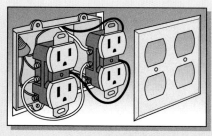

Working on a side-by-side installation is just as easy as a single receptacle. Just remember to sketch the wiring layout.

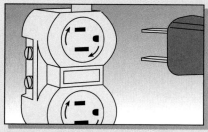

If you have small children, consider using child-proof safety receptacles. You have to twist a cover to expose the slots.

992 REPLACING SWITCHES

Whether you're replacing a switch because it's bad or just because you want a different style the job shouldn't take longer than 15 minutes. And that includes a couple minutes to go to the service panel and cut the power to the circuit.

The common household switch is a single-pole variety that has two brass-colored terminals and (in some cases) a grounding terminal. (Some brands come with grip holes instead of screws.) A switch is wired only into the hot line, with the source feed usually connected to the top terminal.

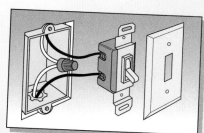

You won't always find the terminals on your new switch positioned the same as on the old one. Here they face the side.

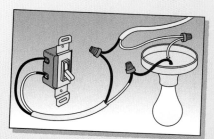

In this exception to the color rules, the white wire in the cable is painted black to indicate that it's serving as a hot wire.

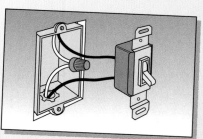

The neutral wires in this circuit are independent of the switch and continue all the way back to the service panel.

173

993 INSTALLING A DEAD-BOLT LOCK

If you want a more secure door, install a second lock. In most cases a dead bolt will do the job. The process should only take about 15 minutes.

After you buy the dead bolt lock, gather the necessary tools: a hammer and chisel, a scratch awl, a screwdriver, an electrical drill, a 1-inch spade bit, and a 2⅛-inch hole saw. (Note: If you don't already own a spade bit or hole saw, it probably will be cheaper to buy an installation kit for a dead-bolt lock. Or you can rent tools from a rental service.)

1. Using the paper template that comes with the lock, locate the centers for the holes you

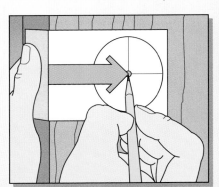

need to drill in the door face and door edge. Mark the centers with a pencil or scratch awl.

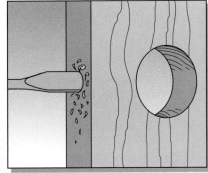

2. With the hole saw fitted into the electric drill, cut the cylinder hole through the door face at the marked location. Then with the spade bit *(shown above)* bore an intersecting bolt hole through the edge of the door. During both of these operations, make sure the drill is held straight and level.

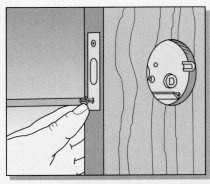

3. Next install the bolt assembly of the lock. To do this, first mark an outline of the faceplate on the edge of the

door. Chisel out enough wood in the marked area to accommodate the faceplate. Slip the bolt assembly into the bolt hole, and fasten the faceplate in place with screws. Remember, it should be flush with the edge of the door.

4. Install the cylinder, the drive bar, and the reinforcing plate and ring as directed by the instructions that come with your lock.

To finish the job, install the strike plate where the bolt touches the door frame when the door is closed. Using the same spade bit you used to drill the bolt hole, bore a hole into the jamb for the strike box. Chisel a mortise for the strike plate and screw it into place, making sure it rests flush to the door frame.

994 USE A BABY MONITOR

A good way to help protect your home while you're gone is to leave a baby monitor at your neighbor's house with the base unit turned on in your home. If your security or fire alarms go off, the neighbors will hear it and can call 911.

LIGHT AT NIGHT

BONUS If you have a pole light in your yard, add a photo cell control. The light will automatically come on at dusk and turn off at dawn.

BONUS Replace your outdoor house lights with lights activated by motion detectors. The last thing a burglar wants is to break in to a well-lit house.

PENNY-PINCHING SECURITY

Keep your defense budget in line at home by selecting some of these low-cost security measures.

Windows

995 A lag-screw system, such as the one shown *below*, can secure double-hung windows. It includes a special key that can sink or retrieve the screw.

Simply drill a hole in an upper corner of the lower window frame and align it with holes in the top sash. Drill holes for a closed position and for partially open positions. When the screw is in, the window won't budge.

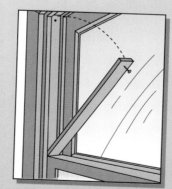

996 A scrap of lumber from your workshop may not look pretty, but it's a free—and effective—lock for double-hung windows. Simply screw the board vertically along the upper sash so that it blocks the bottom window from sliding open. The board must be removed if you want to open the window farther.

997 Keyed locks can also straddle the top of the bottom window. This holds both windows in place. A keyed lock prohibits thieves from unhooking the latch if they manage to break the window. Keep keys nearby for emergencies but keep them out of reach of a would-be burglar.

Security for Less Than $50

998 Security doesn't have to cost a fortune. Here is a list of devices you can install for pocket change.

- ☐ Dead bolts: $9 to $30
- ☐ Reinforced strike plates: $1.50 to $25
- ☐ Reinforced doorjamb: $6.50 to $30
- ☐ Peephole: $1.50 to $8
- ☐ Chain lock: $1 to $8
- ☐ Doorknob: $9 to $50
- ☐ Window locks and latches: Free (a spare screw) or $1.50 to $8 for a key-and-lock system
- ☐ Sliding glass door lock: Free (a block of wood), $1 to $8 (clips or locks), or $10 to $25 (metal bar)
- ☐ Light and appliance timers: $7 to $30
- ☐ Burglar bars: $25
- ☐ Key hasp: $2
- ☐ Padlock: $2 to $25

Keep in mind that security devices work only if you use them regularly. Teach your family how to use them, too.

999 NEW LAMP TIMERS

Household lamp timers that turn lights on after dark while you're away are a good first step to warding off intruders. But movie scenes where burglars predict exactly when timed lights will turn on and off in an unoccupied house are not so far from the truth, according to police. And many break-ins actually occur in broad daylight.

New digital timers on the market create a better illusion of people at home and moving about. Look for timers with a random pattern and multiple program settings that vary slightly each day. Set lights to run on and off from room to room, staging the look of someone moving through the house. And attach appliances like a TV or radio to give the impression that someone is home.

1000 PLANT A BURGLAR BARRIER

Sure you could build a fence but a thief could still hop over the top. If you want security and greenery rolled into one, consider a hedge. Most of these impenetrable shrubs grow more than 10 feet high and up to 10 feet wide but can be pruned to size. They may blossom beautifully but from an intruder's point of view are an ugly front line of defense.

- Arborvitae *(Thuja)*, dense
- Barberry *(Berberis)*, thorny
- Boxwood *(Buxus)*, thorny
- Buckeye *(Aesculus parviflora)*, dense
- Gray dogwood *(Cornus racemosa)*, dense
- Hawthorn *(Crataegus crusgalli)*, rigid and thorny
- Honeysuckle *(Lonicera tatarica)*, dense and twiggy
- Privet *(Ligustrum)*, dense
- Rose *(Rosa rugosa)*, thorny
- Trifoliate orange *(Poncirus trifoliata)*, thorny

1001 LOCK SELECTOR

	TYPE	INSTALLATION/COMMENTS
	Key-In-Knob	Key-in-knob locks install similarly to dead bolts. The latch assembly and chassis insert into predrilled holes in the door. Better models have a hardened steel pin accompanying the beveled latch. Key-in-knob locks are the most common exterior door locks but can be jimmied easily with a credit card or prying tool.
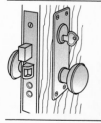	**Full Mortise**	In almost every case, full-mortise locks require installation by a professional locksmith who has the special tools needed to perform the mortising operation. An integral part of your door once installed, full-mortise locks offer double-lock protection including dead-bolt protection. Experts consider them the best lock system.
	Dead Bolt	Adding inexpensive dead bolts to doors protected only by key-in-knob locks is an excellent way to improve entrance security. When shopping for a dead bolt, look for one that has at least a 1-inch bolt. Other desirable features include a hacksaw-resistant rotating steel pin within the bolt and a wrench-resistant, free-spinning brass cover over the outside cylinder.
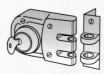	**Rim Mount**	Sometimes referred to as a vertical dead bolt, the rim-mounted lock mounts onto the surface of the interior side of a door. It is the easiest of all locks for a homeowner to install and, like the dead bolt, serves as a good second lock. The rim-mounted lock is well known for its ability to resist prying action.

INDEX

Numbers in **bold** indicate pages with instructive illustrations.